Living Poets

Living Poets

compiled by
Michael Morpurgo
& Clifford Simmons

photographs by Mick Csaky

John Murray 50 Albemarle Street London

It may be that one or two poets whose
work appears in this collection no longer
qualify – in one sense – for inclusion in
an anthology of 'Living Poets'. It should
be understood that at the time the
book was compiled they did in fact
qualify.

This anthology © Michael Morpurgo and Clifford Simmons
1974

Filmset and printed Offset Litho in Great Britain by
Cox & Wyman Ltd, London, Fakenham and Reading

0 7195 2999 9 School
0 7195 3000 8 Paperback

Preface

This is a book of poems for those who enjoy poems already, and for those who have found poetry to be remote and obscure until now.

For most people, poetry remains part of the English curriculum at school, to be studied, analysed – and then forgotten. Thereafter poetry is something that other people read and other people write. Why? Partly, we feel, because it is still the case that too much of the poetry we read at school has little relevance to our own experience or to the world as we see it around us. Very quickly poetry becomes something for the clever people to read and talk about: it becomes remote and dead. So in this book we have tried to bring together poems you will enjoy reading, that will provoke discussion and writing of your own, and will therefore lead you to a wider and deeper enjoyment of poems.

The poems we have chosen are written by living poets of many nationalities and different generations, but poets share the same world we live in, and are writing of experiences and impressions we can readily understand and recognize.

We hope that this book will be widely read by young people and for this reason we have concentrated on childhood and youth in our choice and arrangement. Read from beginning to end, the book reflects the earliest experiences of childhood, moves on to the home and the school, and from there towards a growing awareness of oneself and of the complexities, doubts and wonders of the world around us and beyond us. The photographs are not intended as illustrations to the poems but as Mick Csaky's own interpretation of experience seen through the medium of his camera.

Many people have helped us to compile this book, and we should like to thank Mick Csaky, in particular, for his photographs; and Christopher Copeman, Graham Barrett, Clare Morpurgo, Monica Tweddell, and Jane Austin for their invaluable assistance and advice.

MICHAEL MORPURGO
CLIFFORD SIMMONS

Contents

vii

viii

The lesson

Miroslav Holub

A tree enters and says with a bow:
  I am a tree.
A black tear falls from the sky and says:
  I am a bird.

Down a spider's web
  something like love
    comes near
      and says:
    I am silence.

But by the blackboard sprawls
  a national democratic
  horse in his waistcoat
  and repeats,
  pricking his ears on every side,
  repeats and repeats
    I am the engine of history
    and
    we all
    love
    progress
    and courage
    and
    the fighter's wrath.

Under the classroom door
trickles
a thin stream of blood.

For here begins
the massacre
of the innocents.

The party

Reed Whittemore

They served tea in the sandpile, together with
Mudpies baked on the sidewalk.
After tea
The youngest said that he had had a good dinner,
The oldest dressed for a dance,
And they sallied forth together with watering pots
To moisten a rusted fire truck on account of it
Might rain.

I watched from my study,
Thought of my part in these contributions to world
Gaiety, and resolved
That the very least acknowledgement I could make
Would be to join them;
                              so we
All took our watering pots (filled with pies)
And poured tea on our dog. Then I kissed the children
And told them that when they grew up we would have
Real tea parties.
'That would be fun!' the youngest shouted, and ate pies
With wild surmise.

Sand

Charles Higham

You can make castles of it, construct
The flying buttresses, gold cannons, where
Wind beats down from the sad Pacific –

Make the tall walls elegant and straight,
Carve slits to watch through as the army comes
With stealthy tread across the white, ribbed strand.

Set on the top a thin and tossing flag –
Let it crack bravely like a gun's report
Snapping straight, its linen pressed by breeze

And put the writhing seahorses down
On the drawbridge made of bits of wood from a ship –
Dig out an even moat for the sea to gurgle in.

And finally, when at dusk after a day of labor
You are done, stand naked in the centre,
The only time you can be a warrior –

Braving the sea's clashing shields to ride
You down, your gawk arms raw, a rusted spade
Clutched in your hand, and a drum of heat

Rapped in your chest till the bold green quiets it.

False security

John Betjeman

I remember the dread with which I at a quarter past four
Let go with a bang behind me our house front door
And, clutching a present for my dear little hostess tight,
Sailed out for the children's party into the night
Or rather the gathering night. For still some boys
In the near municipal acres were making a noise
Shuffling in fallen leaves and shouting and whistling

3

And running past hedges of hawthorn, spikey and bristling.
And black in the oncoming darkness stood out the trees
And pink shone the ponds in the sunset ready to freeze
And all was still and ominous waiting for dark
And the keeper was ringing his closing bell in the park
And the arc lights started to fizzle and burst into mauve
As I climbed West Hill to the great big house in The Grove,
Where the children's party was and the dear little hostess.
But halfway up stood the empty house where the ghost is
I crossed to the other side and under the arc
Made a rush for the next kind lamp-post out of the dark
And so to the next and the next till I reached the top
Where the Grove branched off to the left. Then ready to
                                                drop
I ran to the ironwork gateway of number seven
Secure at last on the lamplit fringe of Heaven.
Oh who can say how subtle and safe one feels
Shod in one's children's sandals from Daniel Neal's,
Clad in one's party clothes made of stuff from Heal's?
And who can still one's thrill at the candle shine
On cakes and ices and jelly and blackcurrant wine,
And the warm little feel of my hostess's hand in mine?
Can I forget my delight at the conjuring show?
And wasn't I proud that I was the last to go?
Too overexcited and pleased with myself to know
That the words I heard my hostess's mother employ
To a guest departing, would ever diminish my joy,
I WONDER WHERE JULIA FOUND THAT STRANGE, RATHER
                                    COMMON LITTLE BOY?

Rythm

Iain Crichton Smith

They dunno how it is. I smack a ball
right through the goals. But they dunno how the words
get muddled in my head, get tired somehow.
I look through the window, see. And there's a wall
I'd kick the ball against, just smack and smack.
Old Jerry he can't play, he don't know how,

not now at any rate. He's too flicking small.
See him in shorts, out in the crazy black.
Rythm, he says, and ryme. See him at back.
He don't know nuthing about Law. He'd fall
flat on his face, just like a big sack,
when you're going down the wing, the wind behind you
and crossing into the goalmouth and they're roaring
the whole great crowd. They're up on their feet cheering.
The ball's at your feet and there it goes, just crack.
Old Jerry dives – the wrong way. And they're jearing
and I run to the centre and old Bash
jumps up and down, and I feel great, and wearing
my gold and purpel strip, fresh from the wash.

Windy boy in a windswept tree

Geoffrey Summerfield

The branch swayed, swerved,
Swept and whipped, up,
Down, right to left,
Then leapt to the right again,
As if to hurl him down
To smash to smithereens
On the knife-edge grass
Or smother
In the close-knit quilts of moss.
Out on a crazy limb
He screwed his eyes tight shut,
To keep out the dizzy ground.
Sweat greased his palms;
Fear pricked his forehead.
The twisted branches lunged and lurched,
His body curved, twisted, he arched
His legs and gripped the bark
Between his ankles.
The crust of the bark
Sharp as glasspaper
And rough with wrinkles
Grazed his skin

6

And raised the raw red flesh
And crazed his mind
With fear of breaking.
Then the mad-cap, capering wind
Dropped.
The branch steadied,
Paused,
Rested.
He slowly clambered, slowly, back,
Slowly so safely,
Then dropped
Like a wet blanket
To the rock-like, reassuring ground.
Finally, without a sound,
He walked carefully
Home.

Hide and seek

Vernon Scannell

Call out. Call loud: 'I'm ready! Come and find me!'
The sacks in the toolshed smell like the seaside.
They'll never find you in this salty dark,
But be careful that your feet aren't sticking out.
Wiser not to risk another shout.
The floor is cold. They'll probably be searching
The bushes near the swing. Whatever happens
You mustn't sneeze when they come prowling in.
And here they are, whispering at the door;
You've never heard them sound so hushed before.
Don't breathe. Don't move. Stay dumb. Hide in your
                                      blindness.
They're moving closer, someone stumbles, mutters;
Their words and laughter scuffle, and they're gone.
But don't come out just yet; they'll try the lane
And then the greenhouse and back here again.
They must be thinking that you're very clever,
Getting more puzzled as they search all over.
It seems a long time since they went away.

Your legs are stiff, the cold bites through your coat;
The dark damp smell of sand moves in your throat.
It's time to let them know that you're the winner.
Push off the sacks. Uncurl and stretch. That's better!
Out of the shed and call to them: 'I've won!
Here I am! Come and own up I've caught you!'
The darkening garden watches. Nothing stirs.
The bushes hold their breath; the sun is gone.
Yes, here you are. But where are they who sought you?

Hard cheese

Justin St John

The grown-ups are all safe,
Tucked up inside,
Where they belong.

They doze into the telly,
Bustle through the washing-up,
Snore into the fire,
Rustle through the paper.

They're all there,
Out of harm's way.

Now it's *our* street:
All the back-yards,
All the gardens,
All the shadows,
All the dark corners,
All the privet-hedges,
All the lamp-posts,
All the doorways.

Here is an important announcement:
The army of occupation
Is confined to barracks.
Hooray.

We're the natives.
We creep out at night,
Play everywhere,
Swing on *all* the lamp-posts,
Slit your gizzard?

Then, about nine o'clock,
They send out search-parties.

We can hear them coming.
And we crouch
In the garden-sheds,
Behind the dust-bins,
Up the alley-ways,
Inside the dust-bins,
Or stand stock-still,
And pull ourselves in,
As thin as a pin,
Behind the lamp-posts.

And they stand still,
And peer into the dark.
They take a deep breath –
You can hear it for miles –
And, then, they bawl,
They shout, they caterwaul:
'J-i-i-i-i-i-mmeeee!'
'Timeforbed. D'youhearme?'
'M-a-a-a-a-a-reeee!'
'J-o-o-o-o-o-hnneeee!'
'S-a-a-a-a-a-mmeeee!'
'Mary!' 'Jimmy!'
'Johnny!' 'Sammy!'
Like cats. With very big mouths.

Then we give ourselves up,
Prisoners-of-war.
Till tomorrow night.

But just you wait.
One of these nights
We'll hold out,

We'll lie doggo,
And wait, and wait,
Till they just give up
And mumble
And go to bed.
You just wait.
They'll see!

The astigmatic

Philip Hobsbaum

At seven the sun that lit my world blew out
Leaving me only mist. Through which I probed
My way to school, guessed wildly at the sums
Whose marks on the board I couldn't even see.

They wanted to send me away to a special school.
I refused, and coped as best I could with half
The light lost in the mist, screwing my tears
Into my work, my gritted teeth, my writing –

Which crawled along and writhed. Think thoughts at will,
None of it comes across. Even now friends ask
'How do you read that scrawl?' The fact is, I don't;
Nobody could. I guess. But how would you

Like my world where parallels actually join,
Perspectives vary at sight? Once in a pub
I walked towards a sign marked gents over
A grating and crashed through the floor –

Well, it looked all right to me. Those steep stairs
People told me of later flattened to lines
In my half-world. The rest imagination
Supplied: when you've half a line you extend it.

The lenses drag their framework down my nose.
I still can't look strangers in the face,
Wilting behind a wall of glass at them.
It makes me look shifty at interviews.

I wake up with a headache, chew all day
Aspirins, go to bed dispirited,
Still with a dull pain somewhere in my skull,
And sleep. Then, in my dreams, the sun comes out.

Nursery rhyme of innocence and experience

Charles Causley

I had a silver penny
　　And an apricot tree
And I said to the sailor
　　On the white quay

'Sailor O Sailor
　　Will you bring me
If I give you my penny
　　And my apricot tree

'A fez from Algeria
　　An Arab drum to beat
A little gilt sword
　　And a parakeet?'

And he smiled and he kissed me
　　As strong as death
And I saw his red tongue
　　And I felt his sweet breath

'*You may keep your penny*
　　And your apricot tree
And I'll bring your presents
　　Back from the sea.'

O the ship dipped down
　　On the rim of the sky
And I waited while three
　　Long summers went by

Then one steel morning
　　On the white quay
I saw a grey ship
　　Come in from sea

Slowly she came
　　Across the bay
For her flashing rigging
　　Was shot away

All round her wake
　　The seabirds cried
And flew in and out
　　Of the hole in her side

Slowly she came
　　In the path of the sun
And I heard the sound
　　Of a distant gun

And a stranger came running
　　Up to me
From the deck of the ship
　　And he said, said he

'*O are you the boy*
　　Who would wait on the quay
With the silver penny
　　And the apricot tree?

'*I've a plum-coloured fez*
　　And a drum for thee
And a sword and a parakeet
　　From over the sea.'

'O where is the sailor
　　With bold red hair?
And what is that volley
　　On the bright air?

'O where are the other
   Girls and boys?
And why have you brought me
   Children's toys?'

1939

Alan Brownjohn

Where the ball ran into the bushes,
And I was sent to find it, being
Useful for that more than to play their game,
I saw instead
This badge, from someone's brother, in
Some regiment of that war: a trophy
Begged for and polished, coveted certainly,
But lost now, slightly touched with dust already,
Yet shining still, under smooth leaves drab with dust.
I knew that people prized such trophies then,
It was the way of all of us. I might,
For no one looked, have taken it
For mine. I valued it. It shone
For me as much as anyone.
And yet some fear or honesty, some sense
It wasn't to be mine – it wasn't more –
Said No to all of this. Besides,
They shouted in the distance for their ball.
For once quite quickly, I
Made up my mind
And left the thing behind.

Autobiographical note

Vernon Scannell

Beeston, the place, near Nottingham:
We lived there for three years or so.
Each Saturday at two-o'clock
We queued up for the matinée,

All the kids for streets around
With snotty noses, giant caps,
Cut down coats and heavy boots,
The natural enemies of cops
And schoolteachers. Profane and hoarse
We scrambled, yelled and fought until
The Picture Palace opened up
And we, like Hamelin children, forced
Our bony way into the hall.
That much is easy to recall;
Also the reek of chewing-gum,
Gob-stoppers and liquorice,
But of the flickering myths themselves
Not much remains. The hero was
A milky wide-brimmed hat, a shape
Astride the arched white stallion;
The villain's horse and hat were black.
Disbelief did not exist
And laundered virtue always won
With quicker gun and harder fist,
And all of us applauded it.
Yet I remember moments when
In solitude I'd find myself
Brooding on the sooty man,
The bristling villain, who could move
Imagination in a way
The well-shaved hero never could,
And even warm the nervous heart
With something oddly close to love.

Rough

Stephen Spender

My parents kept me from children who were rough
Who threw words like stones and who wore torn clothes.
Their thighs showed through rags. They ran in the street
And climbed cliffs and stripped by the country streams.

I feared more than tigers their muscles like iron
Their jerking hands and their knees tight on my arms.
I feared the salt coarse pointing of those boys
Who copied my lisp behind me on the road.

They were lithe, they sprang out behind hedges
Like dogs to bark at my world. They threw mud
While I looked the other way, pretending to smile.
I longed to forgive them, but they never smiled.

Boy, cat, canary

Stephen Spender

Our whistling son called his canary Hector.
'Why?' I asked. 'Because I had always about me
More of Hector with his glittering helmet than
Achilles with his triple-thewed shield.' He let Hector
Out of his cage, fly up to the ceiling, perch on his chair, hop
Onto his table where the sword lay bright among books
While he sat in his yellow jersey, doing his homework.
Once, hearing a shout, I entered his room, saw what carnage:
The Siamese cat had worked his tigerish scene.
Hector lay on the floor of his door-open cage
Wings still fluttering, flattened against the sand.
Parallel, horizontal, on the rug, the boy lay
Mouth biting against it, fists hammering boards.
'Tomorrow, let him forget,' I prayed. 'Let him not see
What I see in this room of miniature Iliad –
The golden whistling howled down by the dark.'

Terminal

D. J. Enright

A small boy, four years
Or so of age,
And tired and confused,
In a noisy, crowded building,

16

His ears still hurting
From some mysterious ailment.
He trails behind his parents,
Tired too, if less confused.

Then the people all take sides,
Like in a game,
His father joins the Caucasian file,
His mother the Other.
Which team is his team?
He hears them talking,
His English father, Chinese mother,
And the man who owns the building,

Who rubs his head:
'There's this queue and there's that queue,
There isn't any third queue.
I don't know what to say!'

Neither does the little boy,
He is tired and confused.
In front of him the two queues stretch away,
There isn't any third queue.

Girl with coffee tray

John Fuller

Slipping, she fell into the sitting-room,
For one gay second noticed what was there:
The salmon cushion on the lashed cane chair;
The frail greenness of apples in a gloom
Of chalk wall; round her head the watery boom
Of stool logs, crags and waves of hessian sea
Where driftwood pencils and books floated. She
Considered vaguely that the arching plume
Of her white cat's tail, too, was oceanic.
The sofa creaked. Cups smashed to smithereens.

The cat mewed like a gull, bounced off in panic.
Her feet still sprawling on the hall's wax tiles,
She cried. The seabed carpet stretched for miles
Where she lay drowning in the blues and greens.

The door

Miroslav Holub

Go and open the door.
  Maybe outside there's
  a tree, or a wood,
  a garden,
  or a magic city.

Go and open the door.
  Maybe a dog's rummaging.
  Maybe you'll see a face,
or an eye,
or the picture
        of a picture.

Go and open the door.
  If there's a fog
  it will clear.

Go and open the door.
  Even if there's only
  the darkness ticking,
  even if there's only
  the hollow wind,
  even if
      nothing
         is there,
go and open the door.

At least
there'll be
a draught.

Schoolmistress (*Miss Humm*)

Clive Sansom

Straight-backed as a Windsor chair
She stood on the top playground step
And surveyed her Saturnalian kingdom.
At 8.45 precisely, she stiffened
(If that were possible), produced a key
– A large, cold dungeon-key –
Placed it below her lip, and blew.
No summons from Heaven itself
(It was a church school) was more imperious!
No angel trumpet or Mosean thunder-clap
Calling the Israelites to doom or repentance
Met swifter obedience. No Gorgon
Suspended life with such efficiency.
In the middle of a shout, a scream,
We halted. Our faces froze.
No longer George or Tom or Mary,
But forty reproductions of a single child,
Chilled to conformity. We gathered
Like captive troops and, climbing steps,
Received the inspection of her cool eyes,
Willing them away from unwashed necks
Or black-ringed fingernails,
But knowing our very thoughts were visible
If she chose to see. Nothing escaped her.
She was (as I said, a church school)
God, St Michael, the Recording Angel
And, in our guiltier moments, Lucifer –
A Lucifer in long tweed skirts
And a blouse severely fastened at the neck
By a round cameo that was no ornament
But the outward sign of inward authority.
Even the Rector, when he stepped inside
And the brown walls rumbled to his voice,
Dwindled to a curate . . . . .
It would have astonished us to learn, I think,
That she ate supper, went to bed,
And even, perhaps, on occasions, slept.

An ageing schoolmaster

Vernon Scannell

And now another autumn morning finds me
With chalk dust on my sleeve and in my breath,
Preoccupied with vague habitual speculation
On the huge inevitability of death.

Not wholly wretched, yet knowing absolutely
That I shall never reacquaint myself with joy,
I sniff the smell of ink and chalk and my mortality
And think of when I rolled, a gormless boy.

And rollicked round the playground of my hours
And wonder when precisely tolled the bell
Which summoned me from summer liberties
And brought me to this chill autumnal cell.

And so I gaze upon the April faces
That gleam before me like apples ranged on shelves;
And yet I feel no pinch or prick of envy,
Nor would I have them know their sentenced selves.

With careful effort I can separate the faces –
The dull, the clever, the curious shapes and sizes;
But in the autumn shades I find I' only
Brood upon death who carries off all the prizes.

The French master

Dannie Abse

Everyone in class two at the Grammar School
had heard of Walter Bird, known as Wazo.
They said he'd behead each dullard and fool
or, instead, carve off a tail for fun.

Wazo's cane buzzed like a bee in the air.
Quietly, quietly, in the desks of Form III
sneaky Wazo tweaked our ears and our hair.
Walter Wazo, public enemy No. 1.

Five feet tall, he married sweet Doreen Wall
and combmarks his vaselined hair;
his hands still fluttering ridiculously small,
His eyes the colour of a poison bottle.

Who'd think he'd falter poor love-sick Walter
As bored he read out Lettres de Mon Moulin;
His mouth had begun to soften and alter,
And Class IV ribbed him as only boys can.

Perhaps through kissing his wife to a moan
had alone changed the shape of his lips,
till the habit of her mouth became his own;
No more Walter Wazo, Public Enemy No. 1.

'Boy,' he'd whine, 'yes, please decline the verb to hate.'
In tones dulcet and mild as a girl's,
'Sorry Sir, can't Sir, must go to the lav,'
Whilst Wazo stared out of this world.

Till one day in May Wazo buzzed like a bee,
And stung twice many a warm, inky hand;
he stormed through the form, a catastrophe
returned to this world, No. 1.

Alas, alas, to the VIth Form's disgrace
nobody could quote Villon to that villain.
Again the nasty old mouth zipped on his face,
And not a weak-bladdered boy in the class.

Was Doreen being kissed by a Mr Anon?
Years later I purred, 'Your dear wife, Mr Bird?'
Teeth bared, how he glared before stamping on;
And suddenly I felt sorry for the bastard.

The lesson

Edward Lucie-Smith

'Your father's gone,' my bald headmaster said.
His shiny dome and brown tobacco jar
Splintered at once in tears. It wasn't grief.
I cried for knowledge which was bitterer
Than any grief. For there and then I knew
That grief has uses – that a father dead
Could bind the bully's fist a week or two;
And then I cried for shame, then for relief.

I was a month past ten when I learnt this:
I still remember how the noise was stilled
In school-assembly when my grief came in.
Some goldfish in a bowl quietly sculled
Around their shining prison on its shelf.
They were indifferent. All the other eyes
Were turned towards me. Somewhere in myself
Pride, like a goldfish, flashed a sudden fin.

The place's fault

Philip Hobsbaum

Once, after a rotten day at school –
Sweat on my fingers, pages thumbed with smears,
Cane smashing down to make me keep them neat –
I blinked out to the sunlight and the heat
And stumbled up the hill, still swallowing tears.
A stone hissed past my ear – 'yah! gurt fat fool!'

Some urchins waited for me by my gate.
I shouted swear-words at them, walked away.
'Yeller,' they yelled, ''e's yeller!' And they flung
Clods, stones, bricks – anything to make me run.
I ran, all right, up hill all scorching day
With 'yeller' in my ears. 'I'm not, I'm not!'

22

Another time, playing too near the shops –
Oddly no doubt, I'm told I was quite odd,
Making, no doubt, a noise – a girl in slacks
Came out and told some kids 'Run round the back,
Bash in his back door, smash up his back yard,
And if he yells I'll go and fetch the cops.'

And what a rush I had to lock those doors
Before that rabble reached them! What desire
I've had these twenty years to lock away
That place where fingers pointed out my play,
Where even the grass was tangled with barbed wire,
Where through the streets I waged continual wars!

We left (it was a temporary halt)
The knots of ragged kids, the wired-off beach,
Faces behind the blinds. I'll not return;
There's nothing there I haven't had to learn,
And I've learned nothing that I'd care to teach –
Except that I know it was the place's fault.

Two Sec. Mods.

Zulfikar Ghose

The two boys from 4C who appeared
before the Magistrate for stealing scooters
stand like public statues in the playground
for the adulation of younger boys.

Where their mischief had been ordinary,
they now stamp their high-heeled buckled shoes
during a lesson, ignore the teacher
and talk in his hearing of liquor and girls.

They are tough, quick to unclip their steel-studded
leather belts to swing at other children.
Violence gives them the prominence which
successive years in large classes did not.

24

Lies

Yevgeny Yevtushenko

Telling lies to the young is wrong.
Proving to them that lies are true is wrong.
Telling them that God's in his heaven
and all's well with the world is wrong.
The young know what you mean. The young are people.
Tell them the difficulties can't be counted,
and let them see not only what will be
but see with clarity these present times.
Say obstacles exist they must encounter,
sorrow happens, hardship happens.
The hell with it. Who never knew
the price of happiness will not be happy.
Forgive no error you recognize,
it will repeat itself, increase,
and afterwards our pupils
will not forgive in us what we forgave.

For my son

Alan Brownjohn

Not ever to talk when merely requested,
Not ever to be the performing child,
This is what you would establish;
                          always keeping
Private and awkward counsel against
All coaxing; and going – one hopes –
The way of a good will,

To your own true designs. Which is
The way of some human institutions,
Growing not as any collective urge
                          would have them
(In its own placable image) but into
Their own more wayward value – strong,
Untidy, original, self-possessed.

25

Follower

Seamus Heaney

My father worked with a horse-plough,
His shoulders globed like a full sail strung
Between the shafts and the furrow.
The horses strained at his clicking tongue.

An expert. He would set the wing
And fit the bright steel-pointed sock.
The sod rolled over without breaking.
At the headrig, with a single pluck

Of reins, the sweating team turned round
And back into the land. His eye
Narrowed and angled at the ground,
Mapping the furrow exactly.

I stumbled in his hob-nailed wake,
Fell sometimes on the polished sod;
Sometimes he rode me on his back
Dipping and rising to his plod.

I wanted to grow up and plough,
To close one eye, stiffen my arm.
All I ever did was follow
In his broad shadow round the farm.

I was a nuisance, tripping, falling,
Yapping always. But today
It is my father who keeps stumbling
Behind me, and will not go away.

To my mother

George Barker

Most near, most dear, most loved and most far,
Under the window where I often found her
Sitting as huge as Asia, seismic with laughter,
Gin and chicken helpless in her Irish hand,
Irresistible as Rabelais, but most tender for
The lame dogs and hurt birds that surround her –
She is a procession no one can follow after
But be like a little dog following a brass band.

She will not glance up at the bomber, or condescend
To drop her gin and scuttle to a cellar,
But lean on the mahogany table like a mountain
Whom only faith can move, and so I send
O all my faith, and all my love to tell her
That she will move from mourning into morning.

Little Johnny's final letter

Brian Patten

Mother,
            I won't be home this evening, so
            don't worry; don't hurry to report me missing.
            Don't drain the canals to find me,
            I've decided to stay alive, don't
            search the woods, I'm not hiding,
            simply gone to get myself classified.
            Don't leave my shreddies out,
            I've done with security.
            Don't circulate my photograph to society
            I have disguised myself as a man
            and am giving priority to obscurity.
            It suits me fine:
            I have taken off my short trousers

and put on long ones, and
now am going out into the city, so
don't worry; don't hurry to report me missing.

I've rented a room without any curtains
and sit behind the windows growing cold,
heard your plea on the radio this morning,
you sounded sad and strangely old . . .

A frosty night

Robert Graves

'Alice, dear, what ails you,
  Dazed and lost and shaken?
Has the chill night numbed you?
  Is it fright you have taken?'

'Mother, I am very well,
  I was never better.
Mother, do not hold me so,
  Let me write my letter.'

'Sweet, my dear, what ails you?'
  'No, but I am well.
The night was cold and frosty –
  There's no more to tell.'

'Ay, the night was frosty,
  Coldly gaped the moon,
Yet the birds seemed twittering
  Through green boughs of June.

'Soft and thick the snow lay,
  Stars danced in the sky –
Not all the lambs of May-day
  Skip so bold and high.

'Your feet were dancing, Alice,
　Seemed to dance on air,
You looked a ghost or angel
　In the star-light there.

'Your eyes were frosted star-light;
　Your heart, fire and snow.
Who was it said, "I love you"?'
　'Mother, let me go!'

Sorry

R. S. Thomas

Dear parents,
I forgive you my life,
Begotten in a drab town,
The intention was good;
Passing the street now,
I see the remains of sunlight.

It was not the bone buckled;
You gave me enough food
To renew myself.
It was the mind's weight
Kept me bent, as I grew tall.

It was not your fault.
What should have gone on,
Arrow aimed from a tried bow
At a tried target, has turned back,
Wounding itself
With questions you had not asked.

Grandfather

Derek Mahon

They brought him in on a stretcher from the world,
Wounded but humorous. And soon he recovered –
Boiler-rooms, row upon row of gantries rolled
Away to reveal the landscape of a childhood
Only he can recapture. Even on cold
Mornings he is up at six with a block of wood
Or a box of nails, discreetly up to no good
Or banging round the house like a four-year-old –
Never there when you call. But after dark
You hear his great boots thumping in the hall
And in he comes, as cute as they come. Each night
His shrewd eyes bolt the door and set the clock
Against the future, then his light goes out –
Nothing escapes him. He escapes us all.

Two clocks

John Daniel

There was a clock in Grandad's house:
black, gold-numbered,
and a three-foot pendulum.
I'd hear it tick out endless Christmasses,
fingering patches on the green velvet.

Such splendour. *His* chair.
His knife. *His* fork. 'Wait!'
Grandma would say,
'til your father gets in!'
Twisting my mother to a girl again.

Revenge needs time. 'That junk',
my mother said,
and burned the clock,
the velvet, the Blessed Are the Pure in Heart
in red and gold behind the bed.

And brought him back to live with us.
where bleak electric hands swirled gently,
slicing her days and his
into thin fragments.

My grandmother

Elizabeth Jennings

She kept an antique shop – or it kept her.
Among Apostle spoons and Bristol glass,
The faded silks, the heavy furniture,
She watched her own reflection in the brass
Salvers and silver bowls, as if to prove
Polish was all, there was no need of love.

And I remember how I once refused
To go out with her, since I was afraid.
It was perhaps a wish not to be used
Like antique objects. Though she never said
That she was hurt, I still could feel the guilt
Of that refusal, guessing how she felt.

Later, too frail to keep a shop, she put
All her best things in one long narrow room.
The place smelt old, of things too long kept shut,
The smell of absences where shadows come
That can't be polished. There was nothing then
To give her own reflection back again.

And when she died I felt no grief at all,
Only the guilt of what I once refused.
I walked into her room among the tall
Sideboards and cupboards – things she never used
But needed: and no finger-marks were there,
Only the new dust falling through the air.

Scaffolding

Seamus Heaney

Masons, when they start upon a building,
Are careful to test out the scaffolding;

Make sure the planks won't slip at busy points,
Secure all ladders, tighten bolted joints.

And yet all this comes down when the job's done
Showing off walls of sure and solid stone.

So if, my dear, there sometimes seem to be
Old bridges breaking between you and me

Never fear. We may let the scaffolds fall
Confident that we have built our wall.

Friends

Elizabeth Jennings

I fear it's very wrong of me
And yet I must admit,
When someone offers friendship
I want the *whole* of it.
I don't want everybody else
To share my friends with me.
At least, I want *one* special one,
Who, indisputably,

Likes me much more than all the rest,
Who's always on my side,
Who never cares what others say,
Who lets me come and hide
Within his shadow, in his house –

34

It doesn't matter where –
Who lets me simply be myself,
Who's always, *always* there.

From Beside the seaside

John Betjeman

On a secluded corner of the beach
A game of rounders has been organized
By Mr Pedder, schoolmaster and friend
Of boys and girls – particularly girls.
And here it was the tragedy began,
That life-long tragedy to Jennifer
Which ate into her soul and made her take
To secretarial work in later life
In a department of the Board of Trade.
See boys and girls assembled for the game.
Reflected in the rock pools, freckled legs
Hop, skip and jump in coltish ecstasy.
Ah! parted lips and little pearly teeth,
Wide eyes, snub noses, shorts, divided skirts!
And last year's queen of them was Jennifer.
The snubbiest, cheekiest, lissomest of all.
One smile from her sent Mr Pedder back
Contented to his lodgings. She could wave
Her little finger and the elder boys
Came at her bidding. Even tiny Ruth,
Old Lady D'Ercourt's grandchild, pet of all,
Would bring her shells as timid offerings.
So now with Anne and Michael see her stand,
Our Jennifer, our own, our last year's queen,
For this year's *début* fully confident.
'Get in your places.' Heard above the waves
Are Mr Pedder's organizing shouts.
'Come on. Look sharp. The tide is coming in!'
'He hasn't seen me yet,' thinks Jennifer.
'Line up your team behind you, Christabel!'

On the wet sea-sand waiting to be seen
She stands with Anne and Michael. Let him turn
And then he'll see me. Let him only turn.
Smack went the tennis ball. The bare feet ran.
And smack again. 'He's out! Well caught, Delphine!'
Shrieks, cartwheels, tumbling joyance of the waves.
Oh Mr Pedder, look! Oh here I am!
And there the three of them forlornly stood.
'You ask him, Jennifer.' 'No – Michael? – Anne?'
'I'd rather not.' 'Fains I.' 'It's up to you.'
'Oh, very well, then.' Timidly she goes,
Timid and proud, for the last time a child.
'Can *we* play, Mr Pedder?' But his eyes
Are out to where, among the tousled heads,
He sees the golden curls of Christabel.
'Can *we* play, Mr Pedder?' So he turns.
'*Who* have we here?' The jolly, jolly voice,
The same but not the same. '*Who* have we here?
The Rawlings children! Yes, of course, you may,
Join that side, children, under Christabel.'
No friendly wallop on the B.T.M.
No loving arm-squeeze and no special look.
Oh darting heart-burn, *under Christabel*!
So all those holidays the bitter truth
Sank into Jennifer. No longer queen,
She had outgrown her strength, as Mummy said,
And Mummy made her wear these spectacles.
Because of Mummy she had lost her looks.
Had lost her looks? Still she was Jennifer.
The sands were still the same, the rocks the same,
The sea-weed-waving pools, the bathing-cove,
The outline of the cliffs, the times of tide.
And I'm the same, of course I'm always ME.
But all that August those terrific waves
Thundered defeat along the rocky coast,
And ginger-beery surf hissed 'Christabel!'

If it were winter

Barry MacSweeney

If it were winter
and snowy, I would
build a snowman,
with comb mouth,
eyes of dark blue buttons,
nose of carrot, pipe
of a toothbrush, as real
as 'The Thinker'.
But if you came
along,
      Ann,
asking if you could
knock it down,
after all my effort,
I would say yes.
Yes my love.

And after you had gone
I would secretly rebuild it,
and hide it from you
(not wishing to hurt you).

The rag doll to the heedless child

David Harsent

I love you
with my linen heart.

You cannot
know how these

rigid, lumpy arms
shudder in your grasp,

37

or what
tears dam up against

these blue eye-smudges at
your capriciousness.

At night I watch you sleep;
you'll never know

how I thrust my face
into the stream

of your warm breath;
and how

love-words choke me behind
this sewn-up mouth.

The picnic

John Logan

It is the picnic with Ruth in the Spring.
Ruth was third on my list of seven girls
But the first two were gone (Betty) or else
Had someone (Ellen has accepted Doug).
Indian Gully the last day of school;
Girls make the lunches for the boys too.
I wrote a note to Ruth in algebra class
Day before the test. She smiled, and nodded.
We left the cars and walked through the young corn
The shoots green as paint and the leaves like tongues
Trembling. Beyond the fence where we stood
Some wild strawberry flowered by an elm tree
And Jack-in-the-pulpit was olive ripe.
A blackbird fled as I crossed, and showed
A spot of gold or red under its quick wing.

I held the wire for Ruth and watched the whip
Of her long, striped skirt as she followed.
Three freckles blossomed on her thin, white back
Underneath the loop where the blouse buttoned.
We went for our lunch away from the rest,
Stretched in the new grass, our heads close
Over unknown things wrapped up in wax papers.
Ruth tried for the same, I forget what it was,
And our hands were together. She laughed,
And a breeze caught the edge of her little
Collar and the edge of her brown, loose hair
That touched my cheek. I turned my face in-
to the gentle fall. I saw how sweet it smelled.
She didn't move her head or take her hand.
I felt a soft caving in my stomach
As at the top of the highest slide
When I had been a child, but was not afraid,
And did not know why my eyes moved with wet
As I brushed her cheek with my lips and brushed
Her lips with my own lips. She said to me
Jack, Jack, different than I had ever heard,
Because she wasn't calling me, I think,
Or telling me. She used my name to
Talk in another way I wanted to know.
She laughed again and then she took her hand;
I gave her what we both had touched – can't
Remember what it was, and we ate the lunch.
Afterwards we walked in the small, cool creek,
Our shoes off, her skirt hitched, and she smiling,
My pants rolled, and then we climbed up the high
Side of Indian Gully and looked
Where we had been, our hands together again.
It was then some bright thing came in my eyes,
Starting at the back of them and flowing
Suddenly through my head and down my arms
And stomach and my bare legs that seemed not
To stop in feet, not to feel the red earth
Of the Gully, as though we hung in a
Touch of birds. There was a word in my throat
With the feeling and I knew the first time
What it meant and I said, it's beautiful.

39

Yes, she said, and I felt the sound and word
In my hand join the sound and word in hers
As in one name said, or in one cupped hand.
We put back on our shoes and socks and we
Sat in the grass awhile, crosslegged, under
A blowing tree, not saying anything.
And Ruth played with shells she found in the creek,
As I watched. Her small wrist which was so sweet
To me turned by her breast and the shells dropped
Green, white, blue, easily into her lap,
Passing light through themselves. She gave the pale
Shells to me, and got up and touched her hips
With her light hands, and we walked down slowly
To play the school games with the others.

The railings

Alan Brownjohn

Once there would have been the woman standing
Between the trees behind the dancing railings as he walked,
But that is not now so.

And once there would have been
A hope of the woman, a figment of the branches
As they shifted with the light –
That might have been, that might have been,
But neither is this any longer true.

Not even now is the hope what it was,
And will not regain the face:
Two years, three years, the walk could go
While only the principle of the woman

Faintly remained. And that would scarcely be enough.

The principle will drain from out a place.
The hope will have to go to other things.

Talking after Christmas blues

Adrian Henri

Well I woke up this mornin' it was Christmas Day
And the birds were singing the night away
I saw my stocking lying on the chair
Looked right to the bottom but you weren't there
there was

        apples
          oranges
            chocolates
              . . . . aftershave
– but no you.

So I went downstairs and the dinner was fine
There was pudding and turkey and lots of wine
And I pulled those crackers with a laughing face
Till I saw there was no one in your place
there was

        mincepies
          brandy
            nuts and raisins
              . . . . mashed potato
– but no you.

Now it's New Year and it's Auld Lang Syne
And it's 12 o'clock and I'm feeling fine
Should Auld Acquaintance be Forgot?
I don't know girl, but it hurts a lot
there was

        whisky
          vodka
            dry Martini (stirred
              but not shaken)
. . . . and 12 New Year resolutions
– all of them about you.

So it's all the best for the year ahead
As I stagger upstairs and into bed
Then I looked at the pillow by my side

. . . . I tell you baby I almost cried
there'll be

> Autumn
>
> Summer
>
> Spring
>
> . . . . and Winter

– all of them without you.

Love

Pablo Neruda

So many days, oh so many days
seeing you so tangible and so close,
how do I pay, with what do I pay?

The bloodthirsty spring
has awakened in the woods.
The foxes start from their earths,
the serpents drink the dew,
and I go with you in the leaves
between the pines and the silence,
asking myself how and when
I will have to pay for my luck.

Of everything I have seen,
it's you I want to go on seeing;
of everything I've touched,
it's your flesh I want to go on touching.
I love your orange laughter.
I am moved by the sight of you sleeping.

What am I to do, love, loved one?
I don't know how others love
or how people loved in the past.
I live, watching you, loving you.
Being in love is my nature.

You please me more each afternoon.

Where is she? I keep on asking
if your eyes disappear.
How long she's taking! I think, and I'm hurt.

I feel poor, foolish and sad,
and you arrive and you are lightning
glancing off the peach trees.

That's why I love you and yet not why.
There are so many reasons, and yet so few,
for love has to be so,
involving and general,
particular and terrifying,
honoured and yet in mourning,
flowering like the stars,
and measureless as a kiss.

A small dragon

Brian Patten

I've found a small dragon in the woodshed.
Think it must have come from deep inside a forest
because it's damp and green and leaves
are still reflecting in its eyes.

I fed it on many things, tried grass,
the roots of stars, hazel-nut and dandelion,
but it stared up at me as if to say, I need
foods you can't provide.

It made a nest among the coal,
not unlike a bird's but larger,
it is out of place here
and is quite silent.

43

If you believed in it I would come
hurrying to your house to let you share my wonder,
but I want instead to see
if you yourself will pass this way.

Elegy for David Beynon

Leslie Norris

David, we must have looked comic, sitting
there at next desks; your legs stretched
half-way down the classroom, while
my feet hung a free inch above

the floor. I remember, too, down
at The Gwynne's Field, at the side
of the little Taff, dancing with
laughing fury as you caught

effortlessly at the line-out, sliding
the ball over my head direct to
the outside-half. That was Cyril
Theophilus, who died in his quiet

so long ago that only I, perhaps,
remember he'd hold the ball one-handed
on his thin stomach as he turned
to run. Even there you were careful

to miss us with your scattering
knees as you bumped through
for yet another try. Buffeted
we were, but cheered too by our

unhurt presumption in believing
we could ever have pulled you down.
I think those children, those who died
under your arms in the crushed school,

44

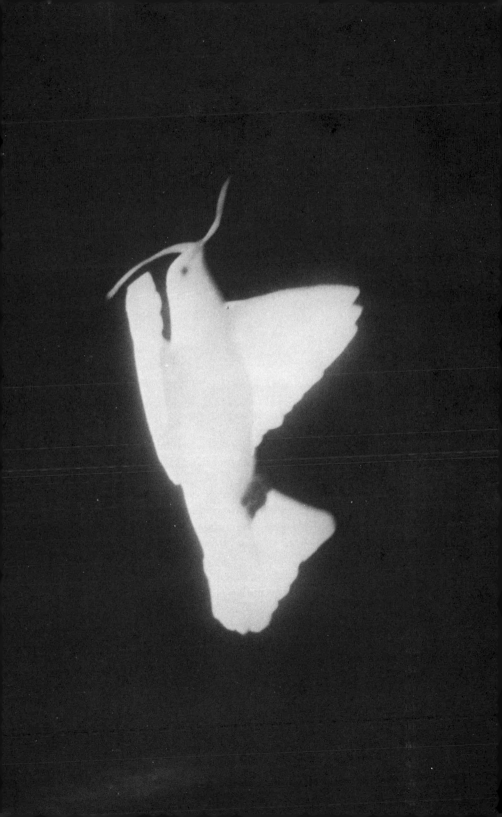

would understand that I make this
your elegy. I know the face you had,
have walked with you enough mornings
under the fallen leaves. Theirs is

the great anonymous tragedy one word
will summarize. Aberfan, I write it
for them here, knowing we've paid to it
our shabby pence, and now it can be stored

with whatever names there are where
children end their briefest pilgrimage.
I cannot find the words for you, David. These
are too long, too many; and not enough.

April rise

Laurie Lee

If ever I saw blessing in the air
    I see it now in this still early day
Where lemon-green the vaporous morning drips
    Wet sunlight on the powder of my eye.

Blown bubble-film of blue, the sky wraps round
    Weeds of warm light whose every root and rod
Splutters with soapy green, and all the world
    Sweats with the bead of summer on its bud.

If ever I heard blessing it is there
    Where birds in trees that shoals and shadows are
Splash with their hidden wings and drops of sound
    Break on my ears their crests of throbbing air.

Pure in the haze the emerald sun dilates,
    The lips of sparrows milk the mossy stones,
While white as water by the lake a girl
    Swims her green hand among the gathered swans.

Now, as the almond burns its smoking wick,
   Dropping small flames to light the candled grass;
Now, as my low blood scales its second chance,
   If ever world were blessèd, now it is.

An ordinary day

Norman MacCaig

I took my mind a walk
Or my mind took me a walk –
Whichever was the truth of it.

The light glittered on the water
Or the water glittered in the light.
Cormorants stood on a tidal rock

With their wings spread out,
Stopping no traffic. Various ducks
Shilly-shallied here and there

On the shilly-shallying water.
An occasional gull yelped. Small flowers
Were doing their level best

To bring to their kerb bees like
Aerial charabancs. Long weeds in the clear
Water did Eastern dances, unregarded

By shoals of darning needles. A cow
Started a moo but thought
Better of it. . . . And my feet took me home

And my mind observed to me,
Or I to it, how ordinary
Extraordinary things are or

How extraordinary ordinary
Things are, like the nature of the mind
And the process of observing.

The one leaf

Leslie Norris

An oak leaf fell from the tree
Into my hand almost, so I kept it.
First in my fingers, very carefully,
Because it was mine. I wiped it,
Put it on my desk, near the typewriter.
Last autumn there were oak leaves falling everywhere.

I could have chosen from so many.
It lay there months, turning browner,
Before I no longer saw it. Now
Here it is again, an old letter
From plenty. From where I stand
This is the one leaf, in the cold house, on the cold ground.

The Chalk Blue butterfly

Stephen Spender

The Chalk Blue (clinging to
A harebell stem, where it loops
Its curving wirefine neck
From which there hangs the flowerbell
Shaken by the wind that shakes
Too, the butterfly) –
Opens now, now shuts, its wings,
Opening, shutting, on a hinge
Sprung at touch of sun or shadow.

Open, the sunned wings mirror
Minute, double, all the sky.
    Shut, the ghostly underwing
Is cloud-opaque, bordered by
Copper spots embossed
By a pigmy hammering.

    I look and look, as though my eyes
Could hold the Chalk Blue in a vice,
Waiting for some other witness
– That child's blue gaze, miraculous.
But today I am alone.

Cynddylan on a tractor

R. S. Thomas

Ah, you should see Cynddylan on a tractor.
Gone the old look that yoked him to the soil;
He's a new man now, part of the machine,
His nerves of metal and his blood oil.
The clutch curses, but the gears obey
His least bidding, and lo, he's away
Out of the farmyard, scattering hens.
Riding to work now as a great man should,
He is the knight at arms breaking the fields'
Mirror of silence, emptying the wood
Of foxes and squirrels and bright jays.
The sun comes over the tall trees
Kindling all the hedges, but not for him
Who runs his engine on a different fuel.
And all the birds are singing, bills wide in vain,
As Cynddylan passes proudly up the lane.

Cynddylan is pronounced Cun-thullan.

Cold

Glyn Hughes

Tonight the brittle trees
rattled and snapped in wind and the stars broke
trembling, like shattered ice.
Logs and frozen heather creaked
and starlight shook under our feet.

My son and I went on to the moor,
walking under drapes of a low room.
A skull cracked underfoot;
a tarred roof winked; a snowball fell;
then quiet, that seemed to glow.
We came indoors when we had stared at snow.

Now we change our places at the hearth
like penguins on an ice-floe. Draughts
enter through wall and roof; the swords
of cold sneak through our warmth
like poison threading liquid in a glass.

Wind

Ted Hughes

This house has been far out at sea all night,
The woods crashing through darkness, the booming hills,
Winds stampeding the fields under the window
Floundering black astride and blinding wet

Till day rose; then under an orange sky
The hills had new places, and wind wielded
Blade-light, luminous black and emerald,
Flexing like the lens of a mad eye.

At noon I scaled along the house-side as far as
The coal-house door. I dared once to look up –
Through the brunt wind that dented the balls of my eyes
The tent of the hills drummed and strained its guyrope,

The fields quivering, the skyline a grimace,
At any second to bang and vanish with a flap:
The wind flung a magpie away and a black-
Back gull bent like an iron bar slowly. The house

Rang like some fine green goblet in the note
That any second would shatter it. Now deep
In chairs, in front of the great fire, we grip
Our hearts and cannot entertain book, thought,

Or each other. We watch the fire blazing,
And feel the roots of the house move, but sit on,
Seeing the window tremble to come in,
Hearing the stones cry out under the horizons.

Fishing harbour towards evening

Richard Kell

Slashed clouds leak gold. Along the slurping wharf
The snugged boats creak and seesaw. Round the masts

Abrasive squalls flake seagulls off the sky:
Choppy with wings the rapids of shrill sound.

Wrapt in spliced airs of fish and tar,
Light wincing on their knives, the clockwork men

Incise and scoop the oily pouches, flip
The soft guts overboard with blood-wet fingers.

Among three rhythms the slapping silver turns
To polished icy marble upon the deck.

Diggle Mill

Glyn Hughes

Bells in their ears; smoke in their lungs;
in their bellies, tea and nettle stew;
high moors as pale and soft as flesh,
and cattle moaning in the dew
they traipsed each dawn; as they returned
traced a snipe or hare through mist.
Now the sheep are turned to shelter
beneath the roof that bred money
to pay for gates of absurd statuary:
this Goddess, fingering with one arm
a coy wrap round her gritstone loin,
who aims an arrow at the lodge.
How could this grass have borne a colour
other than death's white – or black of soot?
The sloes are ripening through October
when rain whips ghosts from the mill's corners
and sways the web of tattered screens,
one door opened shuts another,
draughts slap, and curlews leave the ruins –
no monument: but no-one dares
to pull it down, and it lingers
heroically awkward on the heights
like a nowty gaffer with a loose slate
who fears being forgotten and won't say 'Goodnight'.

Fetching cows

Norman MacCaig

The black one, last as usual, swings her head
And coils a black tongue round a grass-tuft. I
Watch her soft weight come down, her split feet spread.

In front, the others swing and slouch; they roll
Their great Greek eyes and breathe out milky gusts
From muzzles black and shiny as wet coal.

The collie trots, bored, at my heels, then plops
Into the ditch. The sea makes a tired sound
That's always stopping though it never stops.

A haycart squats prickeared against the sky.
Hay breath and milk breath. Far out in the West
The wrecked sun founders though its colours fly.

The collie's bored. There's nothing to control . . .
And the black cow is two native carriers
Bringing its belly home, slung from a pole.

How to catch tiddlers
(*for Stephen*)

Brian Jones

Watch the net drift. Grey tides
Mingle what purposes your eye supposed
But watch the net. There is no fish
Only the net, the way it moves. There is no fish,
Forget the fish. The net is spread
And moving. Steer gently. Keep the hand
Pressured constantly against the stream.
There is no catch now, only the net
And your pressure and your poise. Below,
Ignore the pebbles and the promising weed
Mooning over its secrets. There is just the net,
The hand, and, now, near an old glance somewhere

53

A sleek shape holding its body constant,
Firm in its fluid world. Move on. Watch
Only the net. You are a hand only,
Steering, controlling. Now look.
Inside that silent bulge the shape
Breaks black and firm. You may rise,
You may rise now – the deftest
Turn of wrist will do it. Your hand
Crude again can support the cling of mesh.
You can relax, coldly note
The titchy black squirm. You have achieved.
Commit success to jam jars. Lean again.
Dip the slack net. Let it belly.

The pond

Anthony Thwaite

With nets and kitchen sieves they raid the pond,
Chasing the minnows into bursts of mud,
Scooping and chopping, raking up frond after frond
Of swollen weed after a week of flood.

Thirty or forty minnows bob and flash
In every jam-jar hoarded on the edge,
While the shrill children with each ill-aimed splash
Haul out another dozen as they dredge.

Choked to its banks, the pond spills out its store
Of frantic life. Nothing can drain it dry
Of what it breeds: it breeds so effortlessly
Theft seems to leave it richer than before.

The nostrils snuff its rank bouquet – how warm,
How lavish, foul and indiscriminate, fat
With insolent appetite and thirst, so that
The stomach almost heaves to see it swarm.

54

But trapped in glass the minnows flail and fall,
Sink, with upended bellies showing white.
After an hour I look and see that all
But four or five have died. The greenish light

Ripples to stillness, while the children bend
To spoon the corpses out, matter-of-fact,
Absorbed: as if creation's prodigal act
Shrank to this empty jam-jar in the end.

Death of a cat

Brian Jones

Always fastidious, it removed its dying
From us, and lay down by it in the dark
As if death were a mouse, and a cat's rôle
To deal with it, and not involve the house;
Chose a remote spot that, when I bent to help,
Shocked because it existed – I had thought
The mind a complete map of home; left dust
On my fingers when I had settled it
In front of the fire on an old blanket;
Insisted to the last on standing
And walking with frail dignity to its water
In its usual place in the kitchen, disdaining
The saucer we had thoughtfully set near it.

And death was a wind that tested regularly
The strength the cat had left, and in its walk
Puffed on its flank and made it totter
Then courteously desisted. Death can wait.
Powerless, with crude tears, we watched the cat
Totter and reassert itself again and again
Its life the fuel for its will to live
Until the bones appeared, blood dried in veins,
The pelt was ragbag remnants, the eyes gone out
And the wind's task was easy and the cat fell.

55

The old dog

Alasdair MacLean

Useless.
Our shouts bounce off him.
His eyes, each pasted over
with cataract,
tilt upwards
to the surreptitious claps
that span his days.
The furniture,
he finds,
is still predictable;
the people never were.
Inevitably
we get under his feet.
We curse him and keep him.

Riverdale lion

John Robert Colombo

Bound lion, almost blind from meeting their gaze and
popcorn,
the Saturday kids love you. It is their parents
who would paint your mane with polkadots to match their
California shirts
and would trim your nails for tieslips.

Your few roars delight them. But they wish you would
quicken your pace
and not disappear so often into your artificial cave
for there they think you partake of secret joys and race
through the jungle-green lair of memory
under an African sun as gold as your mane.

But you fool them. You merely suffer the heat and scatter the
                                                              flies.
with your tail. You never saw Africa.
The sign does not tell them that you were born here, in
                                                         captivity,
that you are as much a Canadian as they are.

Conversation with a giraffe at dusk in a zoo

Douglas Livingstone

Hail, lofty,
necking quizzically
through the topgallant leaves
with your lady.

No good making eyelashes at
the distance from me to you
though I confess I should like
to caress your tender horns
and toboggan down your neck,
perhaps swing on your tail.

Your dignity fools no one,
you get engagingly awkward
when you separate and collapse
yourself to drink;
and have you seen
yourself cantering?

Alright, alright, I know
I'm ugly standing still,
squat-necked, so-high.

Just remember there's one or two
things about you too, hey,
like, like, birds now;
they fly much higher.

I saw a jolly hunter

Charles Causley

I saw a jolly hunter
　With a jolly gun
Walking in the country
　In the jolly sun.

In the jolly meadow
　Sat a jolly hare.
Saw the jolly hunter.
　Took jolly care.

Hunter jolly eager –
　Sight of jolly prey.
Forgot gun pointing
　Wrong jolly way.

Jolly hunter jolly head
　Over heels gone.
Jolly old safety-catch
　Not jolly on.

Bang went the jolly gun.
　Hunter jolly dead.
Jolly hare got clean away.
　Jolly good, I said.

R.I.J.P.

You'd better believe him
A fable

Brian Patten

Discovered an old rocking-horse in Woolworth's,
He tried to feed it but without much luck
So he stroked it, had a long conversation about
The trees it came from, the attics it had visited.
Tried to take it out then
But the store detective he
Called the store manager who
Called the police who in court next morning said
'He acted strangely when arrested,
His statement read simply "I believe in rocking-horses".
We have reason to believe him mad.'
'Quite so,' said the prosecution,
'Bring in the rocking-horse as evidence.'
'I'm afraid it's escaped sir,' said the store manager,
'Left a hoof-print as evidence
On the skull of the store detective.'
'Quite so,' said the prosecution, fearful
of the neighing
Out in the corridor.

Warning

Jenny Joseph

When I am an old woman I shall wear purple
With a red hat which doesn't go, and doesn't suit me,
And I shall spend my pension on brandy and summer gloves
And satin sandals, and say we've no money for butter.
I shall sit down on the pavement when I'm tired
And gobble up samples in shops and press alarm bells
And run my stick along the public railings
And make up for the sobriety of my youth.
I shall go out in my slippers in the rain
And pick the flowers in other people's gardens
And learn to spit.

59

You can wear terrible shirts and grow more fat
And eat three pounds of sausages at a go
Or only bread and pickle for a week
And hoard pens and pencils and beermats and things in
                                                    boxes.

But now we must have clothes that keep us dry
And pay the rent and not swear in the street
And set a good example for the children.
We must have friends to dinner and read the papers.

But maybe I ought to practise a little now?
So people who know me are not too shocked and surprised
When suddenly I am old and start to wear purple.

Fairground

W. H. Auden

Thumping old tunes give a voice to its whereabouts
long before one can see the dazzling archway
of coloured lights, beyond which household proverbs
cease to be valid,

a ground sacred to the god of vertigo
and his cult of disarray: here jeopardy,
panic, shock, are dispensed in measured doses
by fool-proof engines.

As passive objects, packed tightly together
on Roller-Coaster or Ferris-Wheel, mortals
taste in their solid flesh the volitional
joys of a seraph.

Soon the Roundabout ends the clumsy conflict
of Right and Left: the riding mob melts into
one spinning sphere, the perfect shape performing
the perfect motion.

60

Mopped and mowed at, as their train worms through a
                                                        tunnel,
by ancestral spooks, caressed by clammy cobwebs,
grinning initiates emerge into daylight
as tribal heroes.

Fun for Youth who knows his libertine spirit
is not a copy of Father's, but has yet to
learn that the tissues which lend it stamina,
like Mum's, are bourgeois.

Those with their wander-years behind them, who are rather
relieved that all routes of escape are spied on,
all hours of amusement counted, requiring
caution, agenda,

keep away: – to be found in coigns where, sitting
in silent synods, they play chess or cribbage,
games that call for patience, foresight, manoeuvre,
like war, like marriage.

Poetry of departures

Philip Larkin

Sometimes you hear, fifth-hand,
As epitaph:
He chucked up everything
And just cleared off,
And always the voice will sound
Certain you approve
This audacious, purifying,
Elemental move.

And they are right, I think.
We all hate home
And having to be there:
I detest my room,
Its specially-chosen junk,
The good books, the good bed,
And my life, in perfect order:
So to hear it said

He walked out on the whole crowd
Leaves me flushed and stirred,
Like *Then she undid her dress*
Or *Take that you bastard*;
Surely I can, if he did?
And that helps me stay
Sober and industrious.
But I'd go today,

Yes, swagger the nut-strewn roads,
Crouch in the fo'c'sle
Stubbly with goodness, if
It weren't so artificial,
Such a deliberate step backwards
To create an object:
Books; china; a life
Reprehensibly perfect.

Let me die a youngman's death

Roger McGough

Let me die a youngman's death
not a clean & inbetween
the sheets holywater death
not a famous-last-words
peaceful out of breath death

When I'm 73
& in constant good tumour
may I be mown down at dawn
by a bright red sports car
on my way home
from an allnight party

Or when I'm 91
with silver hair
& sitting in a barber's chair
may rival gangsters
with hamfisted tommyguns burst in
& give me a short back and insides

Or when I'm 104
& banned from the Cavern
may my mistress
catching me in bed with her daughter
& fearing her son
cut me up into little pieces
& throw away every piece but one

Let me die a youngman's death
not a free from sin tiptoe in
candle wax & waning death
not a curtains drawn by angels borne
'what a nice way to go' death

The face in the mirror

Robert Graves

Grey haunted eyes, absent-mindedly glaring
From wide, uneven orbits; one brow drooping
Somewhat over the eye
Because of a missile fragment still inhering,
Skin deep, as a foolish record of old-world fighting.

Crookedly broken nose – low tackling caused it;
Cheeks, furrowed; coarse grey hair, flying frenetic;
Forehead, wrinkled and high;
Jowls, prominent; ears, large; jaw, pugilistic;
Teeth, few; lips, full and ruddy; mouth, ascetic.

I pause with razor poised, scowling derision
At the mirrored man whose beard needs my attention,
And once more ask him why
He still stands ready, with a boy's presumption,
To court the queen in her high silk pavilion.

Silence

Edward Lucie-Smith

Silence: one would willingly
Consume it, eat it like bread.
There is never enough. Now,
When we are silent, metal
Still rings upon shuddering
Metal; a door slams; a child
Cries; other lives around us.

But remember, there is no
Silence within; the belly
Sighs, grumbles, and what is that
Loud knocking, that summoning?
A drum beats, a drum beats. Hear
Your own noisy machine, which
Is moving towards silence.

Doubts

Elizabeth Jennings

A child, I suffered them. They seemed to me
To show a sudden absence of my God.
I did not dare to look too carefully.
Only I longed to think, be understood.

64

One afternoon I lay upon my bed
And thought of what the Holy Ghost could mean.
A spirit? No, a monstrous bird. Instead
Of peace, the shades began to intervene.

From that day onwards, I could not take one
Doctrine on trust; I questioned each and all.
Perhaps my adolescence had begun.
And I was now admitted to the Fall.

I took the Host and in frantic prayer
Said, 'Yes I do believe, I do believe.'
There was no sign of Christ or angel there,
Nor anything that spoke to me of love.

In Rome much later, I confessed my sins
And heard compassionate words. My faith came back.
Is this how each return to God begins?
Perhaps to know no desert is a lack.

Days

Philip Larkin

What are days for?
Days are where we live.
They come, they wake us
Time and time over.
They are to be happy in:
Where can we live but days?

Ah, solving that question
Brings the priest and the doctor
In their long coats
Running over the fields.

65

Lord of the Dance

Sydney Carter

I danced in the morning
When the world was begun,
And I danced in the moon
And the stars and the sun
And I came down from heaven
And I danced on the earth –
At Bethlehem I had my birth.

Dance then wherever you may be;
I am the Lord of the Dance, said he,
I'll lead you all, wherever you may be,
I will lead you all in the Dance, said he.

I danced for the scribe
And the pharissee,
But they would not dance
And they couldn't follow me;
I danced for the fishermen,
For James and John –
They came with me
And the dance went on.

I danced on the Sabbath
And I cured the lame;
The holy people
Said it was a shame;
They whipped and they stripped
And they hung me high,
And they left me there
On a Cross to die.

I danced on a Friday
When the sky turned black –
It's hard to dance
With the devil on your back;
They buried my body
And they thought I'd gone –

But I am the dance
And I still go on.

They cut me down
And I leap up high –
I am the life
That'll never, never die;
I'll live in you
If you'll live in me –
I am the Lord
Of the Dance, said he.

Dance then wherever you may be;
I am the Lord of the Dance, said he,
I'll lead you all, wherever you may be,
I will lead you all in the Dance, said he.

Friday morning

Sydney Carter

It was on a Friday morning that they took me from the cell,
And I saw they had a carpenter to crucify as well:
You can blame it on to Pilate, you can blame it on the Jews,
You can blame it on the devil, but it's God I accuse.

'*It's God they ought to crucify instead of you and me,*'
I said it to the carpenter a-hanging on the tree.

You can blame it on to Adam, you can blame it on to Eve,
You can blame it on the apple, but that I can't believe;
It was God who made the devil and the woman and the man,
But there wouldn't be an apple if it wasn't in the plan.

Now Barabbas was a killer, and they let Barabbas go,
But you are being crucified for nothing here below,
And God is up in heaven, but he doesn't do a thing,
With a million angels watching, and they never move a wing.

'To hell with Jehovah!' to the carpenter I said,
'I wish that a carpenter had made the world instead.
Good-bye and good luck to you, our ways they will divide,
Remember me in heaven, the man you hung beside.'

Epitaphs

Glyn Hughes

I wade through sea-green grass
to where cow-parsley flowers
'in memory of Joe Bradbury
of Woolroad', overgrown;
and Platt 'inventor of loom';
and Sarah 'relict of same
departed aged sixty years'.
One, whose murder unsolved
local poets renowned,
is crushed by Gothic letter
and careful-careless drape
of stone cloth on an urn
rain-scoured, lead-black;
and lambs take consoling suck
where Joel's 'beloved wife'
who toiled on a high hillside
squabbled, laughed, and cried,
lies now, at last, at rest.
Whose unillustrious kid's
named 'Oliver Cromwell'?
When horses went it broke
his pride; he turned to drink
and left his money for beer
after his funeral.
Or 'Queen Elizabeth Farrar'?
An old man in a pub,
dropping his teeth as he spoke,
said that each day since The War
she sat in The Square. There she died

smoking her pipe and blind.
Now the dogged part-happy life
of 'Sarah Earl, and John
Higson, of Bottom Moor'
spent to shear their sheep,
to card, to dye, to weave,
to carry and to build
is ended. Side by side
without difference
but larger or smaller stones
and rails to rust, they lie
sunk in the unmeasured rain
disguised as epitaphs.
Each year less dutifully brings
the fewer cheaper flowers
and the sexton in his van
who winds the mortuary clock
and watches the new red fields
of houses flood the moor
where Farrar and Earl and Platt
reared half the children they sired
and drowned the others here
in the green sea of grass.

Shipwreck

George Mackay Brown

Paul grounded at Braga, a gull on his shoulder.
The milkmaids wrung him dry.
He lay that night at the fire of Lifia
And then moved inland
And keeps pigs on a black hill.
  Jan put a cut of tobacco in his teeth
When the *Maggi* struck.
They found him at the end of the kirk
Near dawn, out of the gale,
Squirting poison among the tombstones.

For Gregory was much grief in the crofts.
The sea did not offer him with green hands
To the seven dark shawls.
His bones fouled no net or slipway.
With small diagonals crabs covered them.
    Two storms and a dove later
A man with a limpet pail
Turned a gold swathe among seaweed.
That was the hair
Of Robin, weaver of nets, in a warp of ebb.
    Peero said when the first lump of salt
Fell through wrenched timbers,
'Now it seems I can never
Hang a brass chain at my belly
Or sit in the council
Or go among doors with the holy cards' . . .
The gray lumps fell and fell and stopped his breath.
    Peter was three years getting home from the wreck.
He found his feet at Houton.
The ale house there kept him a week.
He stayed at Gair for harvest,
Drowned and drunk again with broken corn,
Then shipped at Scapa
For the blue fish, the whales, the Davis Straits
And casks of hellfire Arctic rum.
He stood dry in his door at last.
Merrag wore a black shawl.
He read his own tombstone that evening.
    For Donald the way was not long.
His father had a dozen horse at Skaill
But Donald loved the dark net.
Indeed for Donald the day and the way were not long.
The old men said,
'Such skill at Greek and physics and poetry
Will bring this Donald fame at last.'
But for him the day was not long.
His day was this long –
Sixteen years, four months, and two days.

Two deaths

Elizabeth Jennings

It was only a film,
Perhaps I shall say later
Forgetting the story, left only
With bright images – the blazing dawn
Over the European ravaged plain,
And a white unsaddled horse, the only calm
Living creature. Will only such pictures remain?

Or shall I see
The shot boy running, running
Clutching the white sheet on the washing-line,
Looking at his own blood like a child
Who never saw blood before and feels defiled,
A boy dying without dignity
Yet brave still, trying to stop himself from falling
And screaming – his white girl waiting just out of calling?

I am ashamed
Not to have seen anyone dead,
Anyone I know I mean;
Odd that yesterday also
I saw a broken cat stretched on a path,
Not quite finished. Its gentle head
Showed one eye staring, mutely beseeching
Death, it seemed. All day
I have thought of death, of violence and death,
Of the blazing Polish light, of the cat's eye:
I am ashamed I have never seen anyone die.

The projectionist's nightmare

Brian Patten

This is the projectionist's nightmare:
A bird finds its way into the cinema,
finds the beam, flies down it,

72

smashes into a screen depicting a garden,
a sunset and two people being nice to each other.
Real blood, real intestines, slither down
the likeness of a tree.
'This is no good,' screams the audience,
'This is not what we came to see.'

Interruption at the Opera House

Brian Patten

At the very beginning of an important symphony
while the rich and famous were settling into their quietly
                                        expensive boxes
a man came crashing through the crowds
carrying in his hands a cage in which
the rightful owner of the music sat
yellow and tiny and very poor;
and taking onto the rostrum this rather timid bird
he turned up the microphones, and it sang.

'A very original beginning to the evening' said the crowds
quietly glancing at their programmes to find
the significance of the intrusion.

Meanwhile at the box office, the organizers of the evening
were arranging for small and uniformed attendants
to evict, even forcefully, the intruders.
But as the attendants, poor and gathered from the nearby
                                        slums at little expense
went rushing down the aisles to do their menial job
they heard above the coughing and irritable rattling of jewels,
a sound that filled their heads with light,
and from somewhere inside them there bubbled up a stream,
and there came a breeze on which their youth was carried.
How sweetly the bird sang!

And though soon the furwrapped crowds
were leaving their boxes and in confusion were winding
                                        their way homeward

still the attendants sat in the aisles,
and some, so delighted at what they heard, rushed out to call
their families and friends.

And their children came
sleepy for it was late in the evening,
very late in the evening,
and they all sat listening
to the rightful owner of the music.

In all the tenement blocks
the lights were clicking on
and the rightful owner of the music
tiny and no longer timid sang
for the rightful owners of the song.

Moving through the silent crowd

Stephen Spender

Moving through the silent crowd
Who stand behind dull cigarettes
These men who idle in the road,
I have the sense of falling light.

They lounge at corners of the street
And greet friends with a shrug of shoulder
And turn their empty pockets out,
The cynical gestures of the poor.

Now they've no work, like better men
Who sit at desks and take much pay
They sleep long nights and rise at ten
To watch the hours that drain away.

I'm jealous of the weeping hours
They stare through with such hungry eyes.
I'm haunted by these images,
I'm haunted by their emptiness.

My busconductor

Roger McGough

My busconductor tells me
he only has one kidney
and that may soon go on strike
through overwork.
Each busticket
takes on a different shape
and texture.
He holds a ninepenny single
as if it were a rose
and puts the shilling in his bag
as a child into a gasmeter.
His thin lips
have no quips
for fat factorygirls
and he ignores
the drunk who snores
and the oldman who talks to himself
and gets off at the wrong stop.
He goes gently to the bedroom
of the bus
to collect
and watch familiar shops and pubs passby
(perhaps for the last time?)
The sameold streets look different now
more distinct
as through new glasses.
And the sky
was it ever so blue?

And all the time
deepdown in the deserted busshelter of his mind
he thinks about his journey nearly done.
One day he'll clock on and never clock off
or clock off and never clock on.

Public bar

D. J. Enright

Why are the faces here so lined?
Have they ever borne the pains of
Poetry? Or the strains of music.
Their hollow eyes have never searched a
Sombre canvas.

Their souls not scorched like ours
By burning issues. Or their cheeks
Trenched by the tears of things. No
Complex loves or losses wrung their hearts
Like ours.

Why do their faces look like this,
Carved through centuries, whole histories
Etched in their skin? Like works of art
Themselves. How did they steal
Our faces?

The hunched

Douglas Dunn

They will not leave me, the lives of other people,
I wear them near my eyes like spectacles.
The sullen magnates, hunched into chins and overcoats
In the back seats of their large cars;
The scholars, so conscientious, as if to escape
The things too real, the names too easily read,
Preferring language stuffed with difficulties;
And the children, furtive with their own parts;
The lonely glutton in the sunlit corner
Of an empty Chinese restaurant;
The coughing woman, leaning on a wall,
Her wedding ring finger in her son's cold hand,
In her back the invisible arch of death.
What makes them laugh, who lives with them?

I stooped to lace a shoe, and they all came back,
Dull, mysterious people without names or faces,
Whose lives I guess about, whose dangers tease,
And not one of them has anything at all to do with me.

The boys

Anthony Thwaite

Six of them climbed aboard,
None of them twenty yet,
At a station up the line:
Flannel shirts rimmed with sweat,
Boots bulled to outrageous shine,
Box-pleats stiff as a board.

Pinkly, smelling of Bass,
They lounged on the blue moquette
And rubbed their blanco off.
One told of where to get
The best crumpet. A cough
From the corner. One wrote on the glass

A word in common use.
The others stirred and jeered.
Reveille was idled through
Till the next station appeared,
And the six of them all threw
Their Weights on the floor. Excuse

For a laugh on the platform. Then
We rattled and moved away,
The boys only just through the door.
It was near the end of the day.
Two slept. One farted and swore,
And went on about his women.

Three hours we had watched this lot,
All of us family men,
Responsible, set in our ways.
I looked at my paper again:

Another H-test. There are days
You wonder whether you're not

Out of touch, old hat, gone stale.
I remembered my twenty-first
In the NAAFI, laid out cold.
Then one of them blew and burst
A bag; and one of the old
Told them to stow it. The pale

Lights of the city came near.
We drew in and stopped. The six
Bundled their kit and ran.
'A good belting would sort out their tricks,'
Said my neighbour, a well-spoken man.
'Yes, but . . .' But he didn't hear.

Fable of the mermaid and the drunks

Pablo Neruda

All these men were there inside
when she entered, utterly naked.
They had been drinking, and began to spit at her.
Recently come from the river, she understood nothing.
She was a mermaid who had lost her way.
The taunts flowed over her glistening flesh.
Obscenities drenched her golden breasts.
A stranger to tears, she did not weep.
A stranger to clothes, she did not dress.
They pocked her with cigarette ends and with burnt corks,
and rolled on the tavern floor with laughter.
She did not speak, since speech was unknown to her.
Her eyes were the colour of faraway love,
her arms were matching topazes.
Her lips moved soundlessly in coral light,
and ultimately, she left by that door.
Scarcely had she entered the river than she was cleansed,
gleaming once more like a white stone in the rain;
and without a backward look, she swam once more,
swam towards nothingness, swam to her dying.

79

Counting the mad

Donald Justice

This one was put in a jacket,
This one was sent home,
This one was given bread and meat
But would eat none,
And this one cried No No No No
All day long.

This one looked at the window
As though it were a wall,
This one saw things that were not there,
This one things that were,
And this one cried No No No No
All day long.

This one thought himself a bird,
This one a dog,
And this one thought himself a man,
An ordinary man,
And cried and cried No No No No
All day long.

In a mental hospital sitting room

Elizabeth Jennings

Utrillo on the wall. A nun is climbing
Steps in Montmartre. We patients sit below.
It does not seem a time for lucid rhyming;
Too much disturbs. It does not seem a time
When anything could fertilize or grow.

It is as if a scream were opened wide,
A mouth demanding everyone to listen.
Too many people cry, too many hide
And stare into themselves. I am afraid.
There are no life-belts here on which to fasten.

81

The nun is climbing up those steps. The room
Shifts till the dust flies in between our eyes.
The only hope is visitors will come
And talk of other things than our disease . . .
So much is stagnant and yet nothing dies.

Visiting hour

Norman MacCaig

The hospital smell
combs my nostrils
as they go bobbing along
green and yellow corridors.

What seems a corpse
is trundled into a lift and vanishes
heavenward.

I will not feel, I will not
feel, until
I have to.

Nurses walk lightly, swiftly,
here and up and down and there,
their slender waists miraculously
carrying their burden
of so much pain, so
many deaths, their eyes
still clear after
so many farewells.

Ward 7. She lies
in a white cave of forgetfulness.
A withered hand
trembles on its stalk. Eyes move
behind eyelids too heavy
to raise. Into an arm wasted
of colour a glass fang is fixed,
not guzzling but giving.

And between her and me
distance shrinks till there is none left
but the distance of pain that neither she nor I
can cross.

She smiles a little at this
black figure in her white cave
who clumsily rises
in the round swimming waves of a bell
and dizzily goes off, growing fainter,
not smaller, leaving behind only
books that will not be read
and fruitless fruits.

Song of the battery hen

Edwin Brock

We can't grumble about accommodation:
we have a new concrete floor that's
always dry, four walls that are
painted white, and a sheet-iron roof
the rain drums on. A fan blows warm air
beneath our feet to disperse the smell
of chicken-shit and, on dull days,
fluorescent lighting sees us.

You can tell me: if you come by
the North door, I am in the twelfth pen
on the left-hand side of the third row
from the floor; and in that pen
I am usually the middle one of three.
But, even without directions, you'd
discover me. I have the same orange-
red comb, yellow beak and auburn
feathers, but as the door opens and you
hear above the electric fan a kind of
one-word wail, I am the one
who sounds loudest in my head.

Listen. Outside this house there's an
orchard with small moss-green apple
trees; beyond that, two fields of
cabbages; then; on the far side of
the road, a broiler house. Listen:
one cockerel grows out of there, as
tall and proud as the first hour of sun.
Sometimes I stop calling with the others
to listen, and wonder if he hears me.

The next time you come here, look for me.
Notice the way I sound inside my head.
God made us all quite differently,
and blessed us with this expensive home.

The Unknown Citizen
(*to JS/07/M/378
This Marble Monument
Is Erected by the State*)

W. H. Auden

He was found by the Bureau of Statistics to be
One against whom there was no official complaint,
And all the reports on his conduct agree
That, in the modern sense of an old-fashioned word, he was a
saint,
For in everything he did he served the Greater Community.
Except for the War till the day he retired
He worked in a factory and never got fired,
But satisfied his employers, Fudge Motors Inc.
Yet he wasn't a scab or odd in his views,
For his Union reports that he paid his dues,
(Our report on his Union shows it was sound)
And our Social Psychology workers found
That he was popular with his mates and liked a drink.
The Press are convinced that he bought a paper every day
And that his reactions to advertisements were normal in
every way.

Policies taken out in his name prove that he was fully insured,
And his Health-card shows he was once in Hospital but left it
cured.
Both Producers Research and High-Grade Living declare
He was fully sensible to the advantages of the Instalment
Plan
And had everything necessary to the Modern Man.
A phonograph, a radio, a car and frigidaire.
Our researches into Public Opinion are content
That he held the proper opinions for the time of year;
When there was peace, he was for peace; when there was war,
he went.
He was married and added five children to the population,
Which our Eugenist says was the right number for a parent
of his generation,
And our teachers report that he never interfered with their
education.
Was he free? Was he happy? The question is absurd:
Had anything been wrong, we should certainly have heard.

Superman

John Updike

I drive my car to supermarket,
The way I take is superhigh,
A superlot is where I park it,
And Super Suds are what I buy.

Supersalesmen sell me tonic –
Super-Tone-O, for Relief.
The planes I ride are supersonic.
In trains, I like the Super Chief.

Supercilious men and women
Call me superficial – me
Who so superbly learned to swim in
Supercolossality.

Superphosphate-fed foods feed me;
Superservice keeps me new.
Who would dare to supersede me,
Super-super-superwho?

Inexpensive progress

John Betjeman

Encase your legs in nylons,
Bestride your hills with pylons
   O age without a soul;
Away with gentle willows
And all the elmy billows
   That through your valleys roll.

Let's say good-bye to hedges
And roads with grassy edges
   And winding country lanes;
Let all things travel faster
Where motor-car is master
   Till only Speed remains.

Destroy the ancient inn-signs
But strew the roads with tin signs
   'Keep Left', 'M4', 'Keep Out!'
Command, instruction, warning,
Repetitive adorning
   The rockeried roundabout;

For every raw obscenity
Must have its small 'amenity',
   Its patch of shaven green,
And hoardings look a wonder
In banks of floribunda
   With floodlights in between.

86

Leave no old village standing
Which could provide a landing
   For aeroplanes to roar,
But spare such cheap defacements
As huts with shattered casements
   Unlived-in since the war.

Let no provincial High Street
Which might be your or my street
   Look as it used to do,
But let the chain stores place here
Their miles of black glass facia
   And traffic thunder through.

And if there is some scenery
Some unpretentious greenery,
   Surviving anywhere,
It does not need protecting
For soon we'll be erecting
   A Power Station there.

When all our roads are lighted
By concrete monsters sited
   Like gallows overhead,
Bathed in the yellow vomit
Each monster belches from it,
   We'll know that we are dead.

The pylons

Stephen Spender

The secret of these hills was stone, and cottages
Of that stone made,
And crumbling roads
That turned on sudden hidden villages.

Now over these small hills they have built the concrete
That trails black wire:
Pylons, those pillars
Bare like nude, giant girls that have no secret.

88

The valley with its gilt and evening look
And the green chestnut
Of customary root,
Are mocked dry like the parched bed of a brook.

But far above and far as sight endures
Like whips of anger
With lightning's danger
There runs the quick perspective of the future.

This dwarfs our emerald country by its trek
So tall with prophecy:
Dreaming of cities
Where often clouds shall lean their swan-white neck.

A removal from Terry Street

Douglas Dunn

On a squeaking cart, they push the usual stuff,
A mattress, bed ends, cups, carpets, chairs,
Four paperback westerns. Two whistling youths
In surplus U.S. Army battle-jackets
Remove their sister's goods. Her husband
Follows, carrying on his shoulders the son
Whose mischief we are glad to see removed,
And pushing, of all things, a lawnmower.
There is no grass in Terry Street. The worms
Come up cracks in concrete yards in moonlight.
That man, I wish him well. I wish him grass.

Number 14

Keith Bosley

That house you took me to
as a child, with its steps down

from the pavements into a doorway
that smelled of damp, along a passage
into a parlour with its black-leaded grate
and a brace of partridge in white
porcelain, that house
where you grew up under your father's belt –
I pass it every day, and up till now
I have watched the street it stood in
fall to the bulldozers, house by house
each day a bit more sky:
old man, the bulldozers have gone away
and your house is still there
its red front door still saying Number 14
its windows hooded with corrugated iron
jagged against the sky; its time come
and gone, waiting for one more stroke.

New block

Patric Dickinson

Three hundred fillings high
The functional sandwich soars,
All the silt of an age –
Cars shops offices dingy offices
Luxury flats flatlets
And sour on upper floors
Milk bottles marking the lonely dead.

Three thousand years down
Through how many Troys and Londons
Archaeologists probe; fragments
Of pots and forgotten tongues
Illuminate all. Why
Must we build higher Babels
The less there is to be said?

The Romanies in town

Anne Beresford

let us leave this place, brother
it is not for us
they have built a great city
with broken glass
see how it shimmers in the evening light?

their feet are bleeding
through walking on splinters
they pretend not to notice

they have offered us a house
with cabbages in the garden
they tell us of their strange country
and want us to stay
and help them fight for it

do not listen, brother
they will bind you with promises
and with hope
on all sides stretch fields of rubble
they say we should admire the view

the young are busy building
new glass palaces
they gather up the splinters
and bathe their feet with tears

come quick come quick
we will take the road towards the sea
we will pick blackberries
from hedges in the lanes
we will pitch camp on empty moors
and watch the hawk skimming
above the trees

but if we do not fight
the hawks will die, sister
they have no time for wild birds
and will shoot us down

Welsh landscape

R. S. Thomas

To live in Wales is to be conscious
At dusk of the spilled blood
That went to the making of the wild sky,
Dyeing the immaculate rivers
In all their courses.
It is to be aware,
Above the noisy tractor
And hum of the machine
Of strife in the strung woods,
Vibrant with sped arrows.
You cannot live in the present,
At least not in Wales.
There is the language for instance,
The soft consonants
Strange to the ear.
There are cries in the dark at night
As owls answer the moon,
And thick ambush of shadows,
Hushed at the fields' corners.
There is no present in Wales,
And no future;
There is only the past,
Brittle with relics,
Wind-bitten towers and castles
With sham ghosts;
Mouldering quarries and mines;
And an impotent people,
Sick with inbreeding,
Worrying the carcase of an old song.

92

This subway station

Charles Reznikoff

This subway station
with its electric lights, pillars of steel, arches of cement
                                        and trains`
quite an improvement on the caves of the cavemen;
but, look! on this wall
a primitive drawing.

A child is singing

Adrian Mitchell

A child is singing
And nobody listening
But the child who is singing:

Bulldozers grab the earth and shower it.
The house is on fire.
Gardeners wet the earth and flower it.
The house is on fire,
The houses are on fire.
Fetch the fire engine, the fire engine's on fire.
We will have to hide in a hole.
We will burn slow like coal.
All the people are on fire.

And a child is singing
And nobody listening
But the child who is singing.

Perplexed by the sunlight

Grevel Lindop

The boy is perplexed by the sunlight:
after four days of sheltering

94

underground, outside the village,
he wanders homeward, to meet
chaos: the dead cattle, voices chattering,
the first fires being relit after the barrage.

Turning slowly above the delta,
the pilot edges over the green map
his silver triangle. Perplexed by the sunlight,
he only half-attends to the navigator,
is half-surprised to feel the cargo drop
and plane leap sunward; he cannot see the target.

The defeated victor

Horst Bienek

I do not come alone
there are many with me
   we comb the forests
   we cross the rivers
   we set fire to their ships
   we blow up their system of underground tunnels
   we occupy the city
      they surrender without a fight
   we disarm them
      they do not defend themselves
   we confiscate their stores
      they do not protest
   we wall up the doors of their houses
      they do not try to get out
   we poison their drinking water
      they sing behind their windows
I shall go away
      But before I go
      I shall take a drink of their water

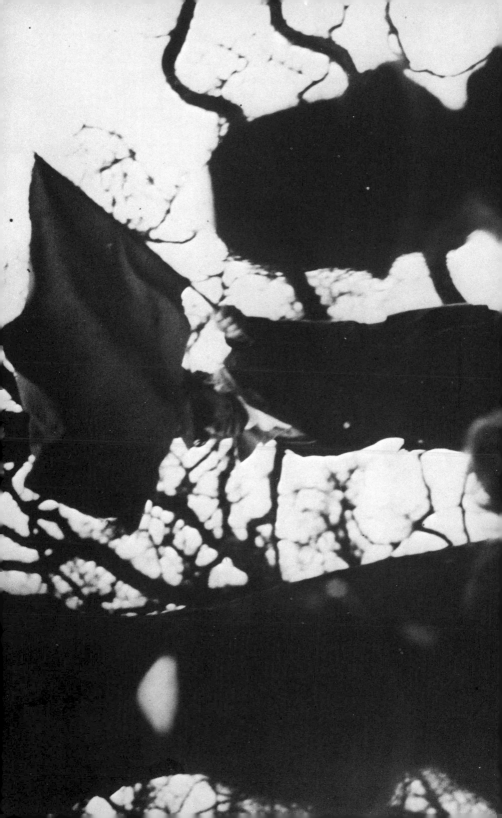

Geography lesson

Zulfikar Ghose

When the jet sprang into the sky,
it was clear why the city
had developed the way it had,
seeing it scaled six inches to the mile.
There seemed an inevitability
about what on ground had looked haphazard,
unplanned and without style
when the jet sprang into the sky.

When the jet reached ten thousand feet,
it was clear why the country
had cities where rivers ran
and why the valleys were populated.
The logic of geography –
that land and water attracted man –
was clearly delineated
when the jet reached ten thousand feet.

When the jet rose six miles high,
it was clear that the earth was round
and that it had more sea than land.
But it was difficult to understand
that the men on the earth found
causes to hate each other, to build
walls across cities and to kill.
From that height, it was not clear why.

The fox

Kenneth Patchen

Because the snow is deep
Without spot that white falling through white air

Because she limps a little – bleeds
Where they shot her

Because hunters have guns
And dogs have hangmen's legs

Because I'd like to take her in my arms
And tend her wound

Because she can't afford to die
Killing the young in her belly

I don't know what to say of a soldier's dying
Because there are no proportions in death.

Ultima ratio regum

Stephen Spender

The guns spell money's ultimate reason
In letters of lead on the spring hillside.
But the boy lying dead under the olive trees
Was too young and too silly
To have been notable to their important eye.
He was a better target for a kiss.

When he lived, tall factory hooters never summoned him.
Nor did restaurant plate-glass doors revolve to wave him in.
His name never appeared in the papers.
The world maintained its traditional wall
Round the dead with their gold sunk deep as a well,
Whilst his life, intangible as a Stock Exchange
    rumour, drifted outside.

O too lightly he threw down his cap
One day when the breeze threw petals from the trees.
The unflowering wall sprouted with guns,
Machine-gun anger quickly scythed the grasses;
Flags and leaves fell from hands and branches;
The tweed cap rotted in the nettles.

Consider his life which was valueless
In terms of employment, hotel ledgers, news files.
Consider. One bullet in ten thousand kills a man.
Ask. Was so much expenditure justified
On the death of one so young and so silly
Lying under the olive trees, O world, O death?

ultima ratio regum : the final argument of kings.

For the record

R. S. Thomas

What was your war record, Prytherch?
I know: up and down the same field,
Following a horse; no oil for tractors;
Sniped at by rain, but never starving.
Did you listen to the reports
Of how heroes are fashioned and how killed?
Did you wait up for the news?
Your world was the same world as before
Wars were contested, noisier only
Because of the echoes in the sky.
The blast worried your hair on its way to the hill;
The distances were a wound
Opened each night. Yet in your acres,
With no medals to be won,
You were on the old side of life,
Helping it in through the dark door
Of earth and beast, quietly repairing
The rents of history with your hands.

Snow in Europe

David Gascoyne

Out of their slumber Europeans spun
Dense dreams: appeasement, miracle, glimpsed flash
Of a new golden era; but could not restrain
The vertical white weight that fell last night
And made their continent a blank.

99

Hush, says the sameness of the snow
The Ural and the Jura now rejoin
The furthest Arctic's desolation. All is one;
Sheer monotone: plain, mountain; country, town:
Contours and boundaries no longer show.

The warring flags hang colourless a while;
Now midnight's icy zero feigns a truce
Between the sighs and seasons, and fades out
All shots and cries. But when the great thaw comes
How red shall be the melting snow, how loud the drums!

Your attention please

Peter Porter

The Polar DEW has just warned that
A nuclear rocket strike of
At least one thousand megatons
Has been launched by the enemy
Directly at our major cities.
This announcement will take
Two and a quarter minutes to make,
You therefore have a further
Eight and a quarter minutes
To comply with the shelter
Requirements published in the Civil
Defence Code – section Atomic Attack.
A specially shortened Mass
Will be broadcast at the end
Of this announcement –
Protestant and Jewish services
Will begin simultaneously –
Select your wavelength immediately
According to instructions
In the Defence Code. Do not
Take well-loved pets (including birds)
Into your shelter – they will consume
Fresh air. Leave the old and bed-
Ridden, you can do nothing for them.

Remember to press the sealing
Switch when everyone is in
The shelter. Set the radiation
Aerial, turn on to the geiger barometer.
Turn off your Television now.
Turn off your radio immediately
The Services end. At the same time
Secure explosion plugs in the ears
Of each member of your family. Take
Down your plasma flasks. Give your children
The pills marked one and two
In the C.D. green container, then put
Them to bed. Do not break
The inside airlock seals until
The radiation All Clear shows
(Watch for the cuckoo in your
perspex panel), or your District
Touring Doctor rings your bell.
If before this your air becomes
Exhausted or if any of your family
Is critically injured, administer
The capsules marked 'Valley Forge'
(Red pocket in No 1 Survival Kit)
For painless death. (Catholics
Will have been instructed by their priests
What to do in this eventuality.)
This announcement is ending. Our President
Has already given orders for
Massive retaliation – it will be
Decisive. Some of us may die.
Remember, statistically
It is not likely to be you.
All flags are flying fully dressed
On Government buildings – the sun is shining.
Death is the least we have to fear.
We are all in the hands of God,
Whatever happens happens by His Will.
Now go quickly to your shelters.

remote house

Hans Enzensberger

when i wake up
the house is silent.
only the birds make noise.
through the window i see
no one. here
no road passes.
there is no wire in the sky
and no wire in the earth.
quiet the living things lie
under the axe.

i put water on to boil.
i cut my bread.
unquiet i press
the red push-button
of the small transistor.

'caribbean crisis . . . . washes whiter
and whiter and whiter . . . . troops ready to fly out . . . .
phase three . . . . that's the way i love you . . . .
amalgamated steel stocks are back to par . . . .'

i do not take the axe.
i do not smash the gadget to pieces.
the voice of terror
calms me; it says:
we are still alive.
the house is silent.
i do not know how to set traps
or make an axe out of flint,
when the last blade
has rusted.

Bedtime story

George Macbeth

Long long ago when the world was a wild place
Planted with bushes and peopled by apes, our
Mission Brigade was at work in the jungle.
    Hard by the Congo

Once, when a foraging detail was active
Scouting for green-fly, it came on a grey man, the
Last living man, in the branch of a baobab
    Stalking a monkey.

Earlier men had disposed of, for pleasure,
Creatures whose names we scarcely remember –
Zebra, rhinoceros, elephants, wart-hog,
    Lion, rats, deer. But

After the wars had extinguished the cities
Only the wild ones were left, half-naked
Near the Equator: and here was the last one,
    Starved for a monkey.

By then the Mission Brigade had encountered
Hundreds of such men: and their procedure,
History tells us, was only to feed them:
    Find them and feed them;

Those were the orders. And this was the last one.
Nobody knew that he was, but he was. Mud
Caked on his flat grey flanks. He was crouched, half-
    armed with a shaved spear

Glinting beneath broad leaves. When their jaws cut
Swathes through the bark and he saw fine teeth shine,
Round eyes roll round and forked arms waver
    Huge as the rough trunks

Over his head, he was frightened. Our workers
Marched through the Congo before he was born, but
This was the first time perhaps that he'd seen one.
    Staring in hot still

Silence, he crouched there: then jumped. With a long swing
Down from his branch, he had angled his spear too
Quickly, before they could hold him, and hurled it
    Hard at the soldier

Leading the detail. How could he know Queen's
Orders were only to help him? The soldier
Winced when the tipped spear pricked him. Unsheathing his
    Sting was a reflex.

Later the Queen was informed. There were no more
Men. An impetuous soldier had killed off,
Purely by chance, the penultimate primate.
    When she was certain,

Squadrons of workers were fanned through the Congo
Detailed to bring back the man's picked bones to be
Sealed in the archives in amber. I'm quite sure
    Nobody found them

After the most industrious search, though.
Where had the bones gone? Over the earth, dear,
Ground by the teeth of the termites, blown by the
    Wind, like the dodo's.

A boy's head

Miroslav Holub

In it there is a space-ship
and a project
for doing away with piano lessons.

And there is
Noah's ark,
which shall be first.

And there is
an entirely new bird,
an entirely new hare,
an entirely new bumble-bee.

There is a river
that flows upwards.

There is a multiplication table.

There is anti-matter.

And it just cannot be trimmed.

I believe
that only what cannot be trimmed
is a head.

There is much promise
in the circumstance
that so many people have heads.

IS THERE A LIFE

Sources and Acknowledgements

Thanks are due to the authors, their representatives and publishers mentioned in the following list for their kind permission to reproduce copyright material:

Dannie Abse: 'The French Master' from *Poems, Golders Green* (Hutchinson).

W. H. Auden: 'Fairground' from *City Without Walls* (Faber & Faber), and 'The Unknown Citizen' from *Collected Shorter Poems 1927–57* (Faber & Faber).

George Barker: 'To My Mother' from *Collected Poems 1930–55* (Faber & Faber).

Anne Beresford: 'The Romanies in Town' from *The Liar* (Rapp & Whiting).

John Betjeman: 'False Security', 'Beside the Seaside', 'Inexpensive Progress' from *Collected Poems* (John Murray).

Horst Bienek: 'The Defeated Victor' from *Selected Poems* (Penguin Books).

Keith Bosley: 'Number 14' from *The Young British Poets* (Chatto & Windus).

Edwin Brock: 'Song of the Battery Hen' from *Penguin Modern Poets, 1966.*

Alan Brownjohn: '1939' from *The Lions' Mouths* (Macmillan), and 'For My Son' from *Sandgrains on a Tray* (Macmillan).

Sydney Carter: 'Friday Morning' and 'Lord of the Dance' from *In the Present Tense 2* (Galliard).

Charles Causley: 'Nursery Rhyme of Innocence and Experience' from *Union Street* (Rupert Hart-Davis), and 'I Saw a Jolly Hunter' from *Figgie Hobbin* (Macmillan).

John Robert Colombo: 'Riverdale Lion' from *New Voices from Commonwealth* (Evans).

Iain Crichton Smith: 'Rythm' from *The Law and the Grace* (Eyre & Spottiswoode).

John Daniel: 'Two Clocks'.

Patric Dickinson: 'New Block' from *This Cold Universe* (Chatto & Windus).

Douglas Dunn: 'The Hunched' from *The Happier Life* (Faber & Faber), and 'A Removal from Terry Street' from *Terry Street* (Faber & Faber).

D. J. Enright: 'Terminal' from *Daughters of Earth* (Chatto & Windus), and 'Public Bar' from *Responses* (Poetry Consortium).

Hans Enzenberger: 'Remote House' from *Poems for People Who Don't Read Poems* (Martin, Secker & Warburg).

John Fuller: 'Girl with Coffee Tray' from *Fairground Music* (Chatto & Windus).

David Gascoyne: 'Snow in Europe' from *Collected Poems* (O.U.P.).

Zulfikar Ghose: 'Two Sec. Mods.' and 'Geography Lesson' from *Jets from Orange* (Macmillan).

Robert Graves: 'A Frosty Night' and 'The Face in the Mirror' from *Collected Poems 1965* (Cassells).

David Harsent: 'The Rag Doll to the Heedless Child' from *Introduction 1* (Faber & Faber).

Seamus Heaney: 'Follower' and 'Scaffolding' from *Death of a Naturalist* (Faber & Faber).

Adrian Henri: 'Talking After Christmas Blues' from *Tonight at Noon* (Rapp & Whiting).

Charles Higham: 'Sand'.

Philip Hobsbaum: 'The Astigmatic' from *In Retreat* (Macmillan), and 'The Place's Fault' from *The Place's Fault and Other Poems* (Macmillan).

Miroslav Holub: 'The Lesson', 'The Door' and 'A Boy's Head' from *Miroslav Holub: Selected Poems* (Penguin).

Glyn Hughes: 'Cold', 'Diggle Mill' and 'Epitaphs' from *Neighbours* (Macmillan).

Ted Hughes: 'Wind' from *The Hawk in the Rain* (Faber & Faber).

Elizabeth Jennings: 'My Grandmother' and 'Two Deaths' from *Collected Poems* (Macmillan), 'Friends' from *The Secret Brother* (Macmillan), and 'Doubts' from *Lucidities* (Macmillan).

Brian Jones: 'How to Catch Tiddlers' and 'Death of a Cat' from *Poems 1966* (Alan Ross).

Jenny Joseph: 'Warning' from *New Poems 1965* (P.E.N.).

Donald Justice: 'Counting the Mad' from *The Summer Anniversaries* (Wesleyan University Press).

Richard Kell: 'Fishing Harbour Towards Evening' from *Control Tower* (Chatto & Windus).

Philip Larkin: 'Poetry of Departures' from *The Less Deceived* (Marvell Press), and 'Days' from *The Whitsun Weddings* (Faber & Faber).

Laurie Lee: 'April Rise' from *The Bloom of Candles* (Chatto & Windus).

Grevel Lindop: 'Perplexed by the Sunlight'.

Douglas Livingstone: 'Conversation with a Giraffe at Dusk in a Zoo' from *Eyes Closed Against the Sun* (O.U.P.).

John Logan: 'The Picnic' from *Ghosts of the Heart* (Univ. of Chicago Press).

Edward Lucie-Smith: 'The Lesson' from *A Tropical Childhood* (O.U.P.), and 'Silence' from *Towards Silence* (O.U.P.).

George Macbeth: 'Bedtime Story' from *The Broken Places* (Scorpion Press).

Norman MacCaig: 'An Ordinary Day' from *Surroundings* (Chatto & Windus), 'Fetching Cows' from *Measures* (Chatto & Windus), and 'Visiting Hour' from *Rings on a Tree* (Hogarth Press).

George Mackay Brown: 'Shipwreck' from *Year of the Whale* (Chatto & Windus).

Alisdair Maclean: 'The Old Dog' from *Introduction I* (Gollancz).

Barry MacSweeney: 'If it were Winter' from *The Boy from the Green Cabaret Tells of his Mother* (Hutchinson).

Derek Mahon: 'Grandfather' from *Night-Crossing* (O.U.P.).

Roger McGough: 'Let me die a Youngman's Death' and 'My Busconductor' from *Penguin Modern Poets 10*.

Adrian Mitchell: 'A Child is Singing' from *Poems* (Jonathan Cape).

Pablo Neruda: 'Love' from *Extravagaria* (Jonathan Cape), and 'Fable of the Mermaid and the Drunks' from *We are Many* (Jonathan Cape).

Leslie Norris: 'Elegy for David Beynon' from *Mountains, Polecats and Pheasants* (Chatto & Windus), and 'The One Leaf' from *Ransomes* (Chatto & Windus).

Kenneth Patchen: 'The Fox' from *Collected Poems* (New Directions Publishing).

Brian Patten: 'A Small Dragon', 'You'd Better Believe Him' and 'The Projectionist's Nightmare' from *Notes to the Hurrying Man* (Allen & Unwin), 'Little Johnny's Final Letter' from *Little Johnny's Confession* (Allen & Unwin), and 'An Interruption at the Opera House' from *The Irrelevant Song* (Allen & Unwin).

Peter Porter: 'Your Attention Please'.

Charles Reznikoff: 'This Subway Station' from *By the Waters of Manhattan* (New Directions Publishing).

Clive Sansom: 'Schoolmistress – Miss Humm' from *Dorset Village* (Methuen).

Vernon Scannell: 'Hide and Seek' from *Walking Wounded* (Eyre & Spottiswoode), 'Autobiographical Note' from *A Sense of Danger* (Putnam), and 'An Ageing Schoolmaster' from *The Listener*.

Stephen Spender: 'My Parents kept me from Children who were Rough', 'Moving Through the Silent Crowd', 'The Pylons' and 'Ultima Ratio Regum' from *Collected Poems 1928–53* (Faber & Faber), and 'Boy, Cat, Canary' and 'The Chalk Blue Butterfly' from *The Generous Days* (Faber & Faber).

Justin St. John: 'Hard Cheese' from *Junior Voices* (Penguin).

Geoffrey Summerfield: 'Windy Boy in a Windswept Tree' (BBC Publications).

R. S. Thomas: 'Cynddylan on a Tractor' and 'Welsh Landscape' from *Song at the Year's Turning* (Rupert Hart-Davis), 'Sorry' from *The Bread of Truth* (Rupert Hart-Davis), and 'For the Record' from *Pieta* (Rupert Hart-Davis).

Anthony Thwaite: 'The Boys' from *The Owl in the Tree* (O.U.P.), and 'The Pond' from *The Stones of Emptiness* (O.U.P).

John Updike: 'Superman' from *Hoping for a Hoopoe* (Gollancz).

Reed Whittemore: 'The Party' from *The Self-Made Man* (Macmillan).

Yevgeny Yevtushenko: 'Lies' from *Yevtushenko: Selected Poems* (Penguin).

(Although every effort has been made to trace original sources and copyright owners there are a few instances where this was not possible. The publishers will be pleased to rectify any such omission in future editions.)

Index of titles

Index of first lines

Straight-backed as a Windsor chair, 19

Telling lies to the young is wrong, 25
That house you took me to, 89
The black one, last as usual, swings her head, 52
The boy is perplexed by the sunlight, 94
The branch swayed, swerved, 6
The Chalk Blue (clinging to, 48
The grown-ups are all safe, 8
The guns spell money's ultimate reason, 98
The hospital smell, 82
The Polar DEW has just warned that, 100
The secret of these hills was stone, and cottages, 88
The two boys from 4C who appeared, 24
There was a clock in Grandad's house, 31
They brought him in on a stretcher from the world, 31
They dunno how it is. I smack a ball, 5
They served tea in the sandpile, together with, 2
They will not leave me, the lives of other people, 77
This house has been far out at sea all night, 50
This is the projectionist's nightmare, 72
This one was put in a jacket, 81
This subway station, 94
Three hundred fillings high, 90
Thumping old tunes give a voice to its whereabouts, 60
To live in Wales is to be conscious, 92
Tonight the brittle trees, 50

Useless, 56
Utrillo on the wall. A nun is climbing, 81

Watch the net drift. Grey tides, 53
We can't grumble about accommodation, 83
Well I woke up this mornin' it was Christmas Day, 41
What are days for? 65
What was your war record, Prytherch? 99
When I am an old woman I shall wear purple, 59
when i wake up, 102
When the jet sprang into the sky, 97
Where the ball ran into the bushes, 13
Why are the faces here so lined? 77
With nets and kitchen sieves they raid the pond, 54

You can make castles of it, construct, 3
'Your father's gone,' my bald headmaster said, 22